A practical guide to changing your career

Work
-a-
holistic

Amalia Chilianis

CONTENTS

INTRODUCTION

Have you ever experienced moments during your working life where you wondered "How did I get here?", "Is this all I can hope for?", "Surely, there has to be something better than this!" or "This is definitely not what I am meant to be doing, but I have no idea what is!"? So many of us are unhappy with our job or career, have been feeling dissatisfied or frustrated for a while, or are stuck in limbo, where both staying in our job or making a change to something else seem equally unappealing. The COVID-19 pandemic has forced many people to re-evaluate their priorities in life, to think about "where to next?" and to figure out how to create a life that they truly want for themselves and their loved ones.

Your time is precious and life is short, so as well as meeting your fundamental need for an income, your work and career can be enjoyable, provide for great satisfaction and work with – not against – your priorities in life. Meaningful and satisfying work can be incredibly rewarding and can positively impact your happiness and wellbeing. My goal is to help you change your career and life for the better through a holistic, practical and empowering guide. This book provides the knowledge and tools for you to change your career or job and to help you to continue to evolve as the world of work continues to change. Investing in yourself and your own ability to transform is safer and more rewarding than placing your trust in one employer and one long-term job.

Work and life are inextricably linked and the action plan for achieving more satisfying work cannot be in isolation from the rest of your life. This is something I've learnt firsthand from more than 25 years in human resources leadership roles for large, complex organisations, including IBM, PricewaterhouseCoopers, National Australia Bank, General Motors Holden, government and others. While at Holden, I designed and led, along with a team and colleagues, the most successful support program to help people transition to new employment post-closure of manufacturing and reduction of engineering services. Although optional for workers to access this program, almost 90% of around 3000 staff participated and successfully secured gainful employment, many into completely new careers. A couple of years after closure in 2019, I decided to go back and interview some of the professionals and senior leaders to uncover what truly made the difference for people when making a career change.

What I uncovered through the interviews was that money from a redundancy payout and working the job-search process were certainly helpful, but they were not the elements that benefited people the most. Too often in our personal lives and our jobs we focus only on working the process and we ignore the whole. It's like creating a diamond to only look at one facet, and then wondering why it looks dull and lacklustre.

Expanding my research to numerous fields of psychology and neuroscience as well as interviews with people from different industries and professions confirmed my findings of what's truly helpful in making a change to work that matters. The good news is there is not one single "right" way; there are multiple paths to success, and exploring facets of the whole from a pragmatic perspective will help you find your own way tailored to you.

To quote the great Dr Seuss:

> You have brains in your head.
> You have feet in your shoes.
> You can steer yourself

> Any direction you choose.
> You're on your own. And you know what you know.
> . . . Oh, the places you'll go!

As in Dr Seuss's tale, another hope and intention for this book is that it helps you to avoid the "Waiting Place" (a most useless place!), whether you wish to make a change or are forced to do so through job loss.

This book provides a practical approach to making sense of a myriad of interconnected research and evidence in a way that is helpful and applicable to a range of industries and professions. It is designed as a guide you can use without hiring a coach or paying for formal assessments and is structured in three parts: "Self and Others," "The Job Market" and "Inspiration," with a number of activities to help you better understand yourself and the value you can bring to numerous possible future roles.

In Part One, "Self and Others," we focus on you: who you are and what you want. We will explore your readiness to change and the things that might be holding you back or keeping you stuck and how to overcome them.

To make any change, and especially if you are hoping to do something really different to what you have done before, then "Pause, Play and Rewind" are powerful tools. Whether you are a convert to the benefits of mindfulness or not, I'm sure you will agree that focused attention is necessary for making significant life changes. The strategies I share will not only help you now, but also at any time when things get challenging or when you need to re-focus. As adults, we often forget how to play; however, play can be therapeutic as well as a great indicator of our strengths, which can show up from an early age. According to Plato, "You can discover more about a person in an hour of play than a year of conversation." Before looking forward, I encourage you look at where you have come from and what you can learn from your experience so far. The Rewind activity on past job satisfaction will be really powerful and useful, showing what you want more of and less of in your next move.

My greatest hopes and intentions are for you to get more of the life you want: more happiness and satisfaction. In "The Whole Picture,"

I suggest a structured way for you to build that picture of your life. Work can be such a rewarding and fulfilling component of life and can influence your life satisfaction and wellbeing. Succeeding at work happens in tandem with the other parts of your life.

Understanding your priority values and how they influence your "Driving Decisions" (sometimes holding you back) will help with your career move, and also your personal life. Finding a new role in which you can regularly experience a state of "Flow" will also increase your happiness and satisfaction. We'll identify your individual "Strengths" and discuss how putting them to good use can result in greater enjoyment at work and better performance with more energy and vitality.

Many programs on changing your career tend to stop at strengths, but your "Capabilities" are your greatest leverage for change. Recognising your capabilities, especially when combined with your strengths, can help you advance or completely change in a way that best sets you up for success. This knowledge will also give you more confidence for making a change and doing it well.

Making the decision and taking action to read this book already demonstrates your "Growth" mindset, your openness to learning. A new understanding and nurturing of this openness will allow you to advance through challenges and to navigate the highs and lows of making a change in order to be more successful, more satisfied and happier.

The idea of having "Meaning and Purpose" at work might seem a little too aspirational for some, or perhaps intangible. We will examine how humans create and seek meaning and how to articulate *why* you do what you do, so that you might derive greater fulfilment from your work. We'll also consider how work can contribute to our sense of "Identity." You'll learn how to create a positive work identity for yourself that will help you move forward, and also help you to reframe any unhelpful thoughts and feelings about who you are from a work perspective.

One of the key ingredients for wellbeing is "Relationships for Support." Close relationships will be important for providing valuable support and encouragement through this change and we'll consider who might be best placed to help you, and the kind of help you might need. We'll also demystify the process of building "Networks" (which can be daunting), by breaking it down into achievable steps and teaching you how to build high-quality connections. Importantly, it will be through connecting with others that you will expand your understanding of the available options. And guaranteed there will be options that you never knew existed!

There's research from environmental psychology that explains how the physical space you work in affects you. "Place" will address how to get the most out of your physical work environment and encourage you to think about the place you ideally want to work in next. "Movement" of both your body and your career will bring benefits outside of the obvious, including being better able to build social connections, which is so important in this journey of change. And in "Bringing it All Together," you'll create a practical career plan that articulates your uniqueness and helps you identify career options and an action plan to move forward.

Part Two, "The Job Market," covers the practicalities of looking and applying for a new job, using the information obtained by the activities in Part One. "Navigating the Job Market" provides an overview of this new environment. There are many roads leading towards your next role and you should traverse them simultaneously to give yourself greater success. A winning resumé and cover letter are explained as two key requirements for the job-application process. I'll also provide recommendations for putting the best version of yourself forward in job interviews and for assessing your job options when you become a real contender for success. And once you know it is a good match for what you want, there are tips on how to negotiate "The Offer."

For some, self-employment is a long-held ambition and could be the best way to achieve your ideal work and life. "Going Out on Your Own" provides advice on the pros and cons of starting a business and where to go to for lots of free help. We'll also discuss how to recognise when a new role is not working out, and how a bit of grit will help you to persevere until you do find the right fit.

In Part Three, "Inspiration," I share true stories from everyday people doing great things. You'll notice that the stories incorporate multiple themes that are addressed throughout the book, demonstrating the interconnectedness of the topics covered. You will be able to relate to their challenges and learn from their experiences. It's reassuring to know that other people have struggled with similar obstacles and have come out the other side more successful, happier and with a greater understanding of themselves and what's important in life.

With all of this new knowledge, you will be best placed to change and improve your work, career and life. Don't waste any more time wondering, "What if there's something better?"! You can start now and achieve something more meaningful and satisfying as well as learning valuable lessons along the way. And as your life and needs change, you can use these strategies and tools whenever necessary. Once you prove to yourself that you can successfully adapt to changing circumstances, you will have the confidence to do so again without hesitation.

I recommend you grab a journal or a notebook and pen and go "old school" in completing the activities. I hope you're excited. Let's begin this journey together!

Part One

SELF AND OTHERS

1 ARE YOU READY?

"Success is liking yourself, liking what you do and liking how you do it."

Maya Angelou

You're here because you aspire to be successful: to like yourself, to like what you do and to like how you do it. You believe – or at least hope – that your career or job can be more meaningful than just paying the bills and merely surviving. The precious time you spend at work should utilise your strengths and skills, help you grow and learn, build rewarding relationships with others and enable you to contribute something meaningful, all while leaving enough room and energy for the other priorities in your life.

Before we leap into preparation and action, it's important to understand and evaluate where you're at: your starting point. Perhaps you have already invested a lot of time into thinking about and planning your career, but you aren't where you thought you would be. Or you've achieved what you were striving for, only to find it still lacking. Maybe you've thought almost too much about making a change and have gotten stuck, languishing and dissatisfied, but not able to do anything about it. So much so, that now you're tired of complaining about your work and others are tired of listening. You may be feeling lost and untethered, recently having been made redundant and trying to come to terms with what's next, especially if the decision to change was not yours.

While these situations are all very different, they all require careful consideration and productive decision-making. What do you want to do next? What's the best way to prepare for a new chapter in life? What's the first step in that direction?

A strong understanding of your starting point and having a few fundamental factors in place will help you to remain motivated and to persevere to achieve your goals effectively.

With a four-year rolling program to the closure of Holden manufacturing, there were initially concerns about people knowing their job would end and what impact that could have. Testament to people's motivation, courage and pride was that quality on production and attendance at work was at its highest ever and the closure became a celebration, rather than commiseration. Humans prove time and time again that they can be motivated to achieve great things, even in the face of adversity, when they have choice, good close relationships for support and the required skills and capabilities to act.

For the Managing Director at the time of Holden manufacturing closure, it personally took some time to be "ready to go." There was a long period of knowing that his time in the role would come to an end, a personal trigger and an ability to have some choice in the timing. In stark contrast, a good friend of his who had a significant career with another organisation only received two weeks' notice that their job was redundant. The surprise, combined with the lack of choice and time to prepare, made for a much more difficult and negative experience. I've witnessed and personally experienced this latter scenario when a redundancy or change in job has come out of the blue. Not only does the surprise affect your emotions and ability to respond, it can also come with a side serve of self-doubt and questioning, which can affect your confidence.

Motivation and confidence will be critical to your starting point and to beginning this journey. Motivation is a personal, internal condition that drives change and the pursuit of goals. Psychologists have shown that three factors best facilitate and enable motivation: (1) autonomy (i.e., having some control over a situation), (2) a sense of belonging and (3) feeling competent.[1] This is sometimes referred to by the acronym "ABC" (autonomy, belonging and competence). In this context of changing your career or job, your motivation to change and succeed will rely on: (1) your belief that you have a choice (whether it is choosing to make a change or choosing how to respond to a given situation), (2) your supportive relationships and (3) a specific set of skills that will enable you to make the change.

Although many people may have the motivation to make a change – that is, they have choice, support and skills – it can be their confidence in their skills and ability that can either accelerate or halt their action. One of my clients worked for a major retailer in the head office for over 20 years. She was given almost a year's notice that her role would cease to exist and had the option to take her redundancy payment and leave at a time of her choosing, if and when she found another job. I worked with her and she gained the ability and skills to present herself well in her resumé, cover letter and in interview. She applied for just one job and was invited for interview. Although nervous, she did her absolute best and was proud of how she had performed. After hearing that she was unsuccessful, she stopped applying for jobs. Then COVID-19 hit, and you can surmise the rest. She had a great skill set and experience in an area that not a lot of people possess, demonstrated loyalty and commitment and a strong work ethic. All the factors for motivation existed, but it was her confidence that stopped her from taking a risk and applying for more jobs. When you have been out of practice in applying for jobs, or enter the job market after a long period of time, it can be daunting to learn how to promote yourself, talk about your successes and then potentially experience failure. The good news is, you can learn how to do this, build your confidence and obtain the skills and knowledge for when you need to do it again in the future.

If you suspect that your motivation is high, but that your confidence may hold you back, this book incorporates many strategies that will help you build your confidence. You'll be encouraged to take small, safe steps. I'll provide guidance on who to choose to help support you through this change, and you will learn how failure and risk taking can lead to growth and insight. As you try the activities, effectively testing and learning as you go, your confidence will build. And even if confidence is not an issue for you, these strategies will also help with resilience and wellbeing: lifelong tools.

In an interview, the former Managing Director of Holden likened the emotional connection to a job to a romantic relationship: the length of time invested, the fear of the unknown and being ready to let go and move on to someone new, even when you know that the relationship has its flaws. Possibly we can all relate to that relationship we know we stayed in for too long, but there were a range of reasons that we justified to ourselves for not deciding to make a change.

Psychologists have long studied judgement and decision-making. Humans make decisions in two distinct ways: consciously and analytically, or unconsciously using our "gut," intuition or instinct (although both depend on the brain).[2] However, before anyone makes a decision and takes action, they will contemplate or think about the situation in order to come to a decision, prepare, and then take action. To make a successful change to your career or job requires both types of decision-making and definitely needs high motivation, good preparation, confidence and a lot of action.

Figure 1: Judgement and Decision-Making

In this current environment of uncertainty and economic challenges, everyone's sense of control is impacted and the future is uncertain. However, you can take steps to pragmatically and effectively move forward.

The following activities are designed to help you process your thoughts and feelings about where you are now with your motivation and confidence in making a change. As an added benefit, when you begin to take action and the process of making a change perhaps becomes difficult or anxiety creeps in, reviewing these activities will help keep you moving forward.

ACTIVITY 1

Readiness Review

To help you better understand your starting point, I recommend reviewing your motivation and your confidence. Review Table 1 and write your answers in a journal or notebook. To make the most of the activities to come, they are best captured in a dedicated journal, notebook or folder, enabling you to build on each activity as you go.

Table 1: Readiness Review

CHOICE	SUPPORT	ABILITY	CONFIDENCE
Do you believe you have the freedom to choose to make a change?	Do you have close relationships for support?	What is your current knowledge and ability about what career/job to change to and how?	On a scale of 0 to 5, how confident are you that you have what it takes to make a career change?
• Reflect and answer the above. • Where you feel there is no choice, write down what you can and can't control about those reasons.	• Reflect and answer the above. • Are there concerns from those closest to you that are helping or hindering you from making the change you hope for?	• Do you have a clear idea of what is next? • In the career change process, what do you think you are already pretty good at? • What do you know you need to learn?	• Does worry or rumination stop you from acting? • Are you too focused on pleasing others which stops you? • Do you think you need to be perfect for that next job or career before you go for it?

Motivation

By reflecting on these questions, you will be better placed to understand your motivation and confidence levels. This might seem obvious; or you might be forced to make a change, so it might seem irrelevant. But it's not.

Let's look at each component and why. Psychologists have found that autonomy (having a choice or some control) is a basic psychological need for motivation. If you don't believe you have a choice, you might find yourself applying for jobs and going through interviews, and others will be able to read the signs of your lack of inner motivation, even if you are not conscious of it. You will be better placed to navigate both the highs and lows of changing careers or jobs when you have the right people for support and Chapter 11 is dedicated to this. The intention of this book is to help you gain clarity on what's next and then how to navigate the job market to achieve it. If you are already pretty good at that, then great; if not, keep reading.

Confidence is a big topic. There are entire books dedicated to it. Asking you to assign a rating to how confident you feel helps to explain where you are at right now. Potentially it uncovers useful data about what might be holding you back, to help you move on from the "Waiting Place," if that is where you have been for some time. The Waiting Place, as described by Dr Seuss, is "a most useless place". In this context, it sees you waiting for something, anything, to happen to force you to act, rather than you deciding for yourself. If worry, people pleasing or perfectionism are impacting your confidence and ability to act, then acknowledging this is a great first step. Look at the things that are worrying you, what you fear. What is the likelihood that the worst-case scenario would actually happen? For example, you are worried about paying your bills and making a change might mean less money. First, is this true? Really true? Perhaps you are *assuming* that the change comes with less money and have not actually validated that this is the case. Perhaps there are ways to set yourself up with a side hustle, minimising the income gap. Second, how likely is it that you will throw caution to the wind and do something so reckless that it leaves you financially devastated?

If your worries or fears are about your own perceived lack of ability, then try to imagine it is a very good friend, or perhaps your own child as an adult, coming to you with those same concerns. What would you say to them? How would you help them? I'm encouraging you to be as kind and encouraging to yourself as you would be to others. Keep track of any of these negative thoughts and use these questions and the ones above to catch them and test how true they really are.

Encouraging small safe steps will both build your confidence and give you check-in points to catch your fears and most likely prove that they were just fears, passing thoughts, and not psychic predictions.

One thing to watch for is whether your perception of "confidence" (and what that looks like) requires behaviours that are not authentically you. You don't have to pretend to be something you are not to be confident. It is not about "faking it until you make it." Studies show that perception is changing and has changed for what traits people value in leadership.[3] Confidence is really about your ability to lead yourself. Flexible, patient, collaborative, loyal, empathetic, reasonable and more are what people want in leaders. If your view of confidence is associated with being aggressive and dominant, then the good news is you can let go of this view. Your path forward involves being authentically you, becoming confident in your skills and capabilities and learning how to promote yourself and the value you can deliver.

ACTIVITY 2

It's Not Me, It's You

Another way to further understand your readiness to change your job or career is to think about it as a relationship. In your journal, reflect on and capture how you would describe your current work or job if it were a relationship.

Would it be a relationship you'd introduce to your family or best friend? How would you introduce them? Would your family or friend say they (your work/employer) treat you well? What are the qualities you value the most? What are the qualities you value the least, that frustrate or upset you?

Making a change is not easy, but can deliver great rewards. Distancing yourself by using an analogy like a relationship can give you a new perspective and insights that help with your motivation to stay or go. Even if you have been forced to change your job, this exercise is worth doing as a way of processing what has happened.

While this book is designed for use without paying for additional expertise or advice (although please do so if you choose to), you will be asked to choose one or two supportive relationships to assist you with navigating the highs and lows of making a change. These relationships will hopefully allow you to talk through some of the activities and your progress, to understand any missteps or mistakes as learning experiences, and to have open, honest and respectful discussions with an occasional mirror of truth held up (even when you don't want it!). Different types of connections and relationships for support are explored in later chapters and importantly how to be selective with who you trust for help. Like starting a road trip by checking your oil levels, tyre pressure, even water for the windscreen wipers, we're making sure that you are well prepared for the journey ahead. Your motivation, confidence and decisions to act are your first keys to making a successful change to your career or job. While parts of the journey cover the unknown, we're building on the exciting road ahead, what will be gained from the journey and where it will take you. Next, we look at "Pause, Play and Rewind" as strategies to help you begin to gain clarity and further overcome any stumbling blocks.

2 PAUSE, PLAY AND REWIND

If you want to avoid the rinse-and-repeat cycle that brings you to the end of your working life troubled by regrets of "could of," "should of" and "wonder if," then you need to pause, play and rewind. If you want to lose that Sunday evening dread at the thought of starting another week of more of the same – work, home, responsibilities, sleep and get up and do it all over again – then you need time out. And if you are out of work, and the stressors of the job-search process and concerns about financial security are making you experience negative thoughts or feel nervous or anxious, then it is equally if not more important for you.

Taking time out may seem counterintuitive, as most career coaches will tell you that the job-search process is like running a race: the sooner you start the sooner you reach your destination. However, if you want to run that race with a clear goal and perform at your best, pause, play and rewind will give you the tools you need.

The health crisis of 2020 forced many people and industries to pause. This forced stop at some point can be an opportunity to re-evaluate and re-set. If you look back on your working life so far, have you just gone along for the ride? Have you ever had a real break to stop thinking about pressures, expectations, judgements and responsibilities? Particularly if you are hoping to do something different from what you have been doing up until this point, it's important to stop for a moment.

You might intuitively know this to be true. It's often those times when you are not thinking about a problem or a challenge that solutions come to you. This could happen when you are in the shower, playing sport, or in an exercise class: a new idea seems to come from somewhere outside of you and points a way forward.

WHY MINDFULNESS? PAUSE FOR FOCUSED ATTENTION

Mindfulness is training the mind for focused attention and this state of mind helps you gain clarity and perform at your best to reach your potential.

You are capable of making a change successfully and you have strengths, capabilities and the ability to learn. And, undoubtedly, you have made successful changes in your past, overcome obstacles and achieved your desired goals, from finishing school or university, to moving or buying a home, building lasting relationships and securing work of some kind.

With making this change that is ahead of you, you increase your chances of success by understanding how your brain works, when it will interfere with your performance and how to address and reduce these hindrances. The skills you need to perform at your best, such as planning, organising, processing information, problem-solving and decision-making, are largely performed in one area of the brain, the prefrontal cortex. For optimal functioning, much like a battery, the brain needs to be fully charged with sleep and nutrition; it becomes worn down when overused (aka daily life). For human survival, there is another part of the brain that will "hijack" the prefrontal cortex when we perceive we are under threat. And while we are no longer chased by flesh-eating predators (well, most of the time!), we might still find ourselves in "threatening" situations (e.g., during the job-search process or even in our daily work) that cause this same biological reaction: a fight, flight or freeze response.

Your best strategy, from a neuroscientific and biological perspective, is to reduce the activation of your amygdala (part of the brain responsible for the fight, flight or freeze response) and boost your ability to think, plan and respond. Science has proven that, when practised regularly, mindfulness reduces the size of your amygdala and therefore reduces your nerves, anxiety and negative thoughts. It also provides long-term benefits, such as increased creativity, cognitive and physical performance, focus, decision-making and wellbeing.

Addressing negative thoughts is crucial. Like taxes, they are unavoidable, and we all respond to them, but this strategy of being aware of them, choosing how to respond and reducing how often they occur will help you address any worries, fears, or issues with confidence that Activity 1 may have helped you identify.

THE "HOW" OF MINDFULNESS

You may be someone who is already reaping the benefits of a regular mindfulness practice, such as meditation. Or you might be turned off by the term "mindfulness" and shudder at the thought of meditating, being still and paying attention to your thoughts. Meditation is one scientifically proven way to achieve the state of mindfulness, focused attention, but it is not the only way.

We have all experienced that voice in our head that is constantly chatting, telling you what to do, think and feel. This can be described as your automatic or default setting. Humans have over 6000 thoughts every day; this average of being interrupted every 14.4 seconds is a constant distraction that hinders your ability to focus, and impacts how you feel and whether you act. Therefore, you need to quieten this voice and mindfulness does this by bringing attention to one of your five senses: sight, hearing, smell, taste or touch.

With regular practice, mindfulness trains the mind to become better at focusing your attention. It allows you to be present, in the here and now, and to place a pause between your thoughts and actions. While practising mindfulness, thoughts will be present and we learn how to notice them and to consciously respond, rather than react. I enjoy meditation as a way of achieving mindfulness; but you can achieve the benefits of mindfulness in a number of ways. Take something that you already do, a mundane chore like washing the dishes. Instead of letting your mind wander and think through your endless to-do list, focus on the task. Check in with your senses, notice what you see, smell and feel. Your mind might wander and that is ok. Thank the thought for coming, and in your mind push it to the side to address at another time. Focus back on what you were doing.

If you don't already meditate and are open to trying it, I recommend starting with a short, guided meditation from a free app. Insight Timer has the world's largest free library of meditations and other resources and can be filtered according to when and why you are using it (e.g., morning, sleep or confidence) and how long you have to meditate. Even starting with five minutes and building up to a regular practice of ten to fifteen minutes daily will deliver long-term benefits.

If meditation is still not for you, then there are other practices that can cultivate mindfulness (such as yoga or tai chi) or, as suggested earlier, by simply incorporating focused attention into routine daily actions, such as taking a shower, washing dishes, or savouring what you eat. Find something that works for you and try it more than once. Sometimes these practices can be uncomfortable at first, but over time, the benefits that result transform it into an experience that you look forward to.

YOUR "ON-THE-SPOT" STRATEGY

If during your journey ahead you experience nervousness, anxiety or negative unhelpful thoughts, you now know your amygdala has been activated. Practising mindfulness will reduce this activation, but when it does happen, the key will be to calm it down. You don't need to eradicate these feelings; what you need is a strategy that stops them from taking over and impeding your ability to perform. It has been found that breathing out is the part of the breath that calms you down. Therefore, taking in deep breaths and an even longer exhale will help you calm your nervous system when you are stressed. Try a deep inhalation to the count of four, pause (hold your breath for the count of four) and then slowly exhale for the count of five. This longer exhale will calm your nerves and can be easily practised any time you feel stressed.

ACTIVITY 3

Start a Regular Mindfulness Practice

Choose a practice that cultivates mindfulness, whether that be meditation, yoga, tai chi, or a small daily practice attached to part of your routine. After your practice, write down in your journal any thoughts, feelings and a description of the experience, all without judgement. You may be surprised by what you notice, how you feel and what thoughts are showing up. Feelings and emotions are data. Ignoring them is like making a decision based on only half the facts. If something makes you envious or jealous, it signals perhaps that someone else is doing something that you would like to do. If something makes you angry, rather than respond, write down why you think that is.

If the neuroscience and biology still don't convince you to pause and you just want to get straight to the process and the plan, all I ask is that you give it a try. This has relevance and I have observed and personally experienced on a number of occasions that when people ignore their physical, emotional and mental signals, the body has a way of forcing them to stop.

PLAY

Play has made a crucial contribution to human development, the history of human survival and our ability to adapt. Humans have the capacity to generate new neurons throughout our lives. We are neotenous: that is, we retain a juvenile ability to play. Perhaps social conditioning and the complexity of modern life have reduced our focus on play as adults. We've made it a differential – either we work or we play – and as we age, there is often less time for such frivolous, pointless activities.

Research on the benefits of play is not limited to children. Similar to mindfulness, play has been proven to have an incredible number of developmental benefits, such as a way to improve problem-solving, creativity, language, self-regulation and social skills.

"You can discover more about a person in an hour of play than a year of conversation."

Plato

Dr Stuart Brown is the founder of the National Institute for Play, and is trained in medicine, psychiatry and clinical research. For Brown, play is not just therapeutic, it is diagnostic; people's early experiences of play are addressed in clinical settings to learn a lot about them in a short time. In his book, *Play: How it Shapes the Brain, Opens the Imagination and Invigorates the Soul* (2010), he prefers to *describe* play rather than define it.[1] There is no single definition of "play" that all researchers, clinicians and therapists agree on; however, there are common characteristics that describe play. You choose to do it, make your own decisions and enjoy the act, there are both rules and room for creativity; it is imaginative and conducted in an active, but relatively non-stressed, frame of mind.

Perhaps we've created an incorrect societal norm that work and play are mutually exclusive. Looking at the characteristics of play, there are times in our work where we have had opportunities to be imaginative and creative and to try something for its own reward. Maybe this has happened for you as part of a training program, a team day, problem-solving, an induction program, when starting a new job, brainstorming a new product or solution or simply socialising with colleagues based around a group activity, such as bowling or mini golf.

In his TED Talk, "Play is More Than Just Having Fun," Brown describes a Play History activity. Building on this concept, the following activity will unpack your early experiences of play to understand more about what you enjoy doing and in what context.

ACTIVITY 4

Play History

Sitting or standing in a quiet space, think back through your earliest memories and recall the most clear, joyful, playful image that you can. Perhaps you were playing with your favourite toy, at a party, on holiday, reading books, building something or playing a game. Describe the memory. Think about all of the senses: how it looked, sounded, smelled, tasted and felt. What were you doing? What emotions were present? What was it about that experience that led to positive emotions for you?

How does that compare to what you do now, in your work and life? Are there activities in your current experience that provide you with similar joy?

Brown doesn't recommend differentiating work from play, but rather finding ways to incorporate play into your everyday routine in order to enrich your life by prioritising and paying attention to it. Appreciate and recognise where you do have opportunities for play in your current work and life and if there are not enough opportunities for play, then create at least one. Perhaps your moments for play will also bring opportunities for mindfulness through focused attention on one of your five senses.

As you progress through the chapters that follow, you may notice some consistent elements that tie back to this activity in a way you may not have previously considered.

REWIND

Before we look ahead to the change you hope to make, it's helpful to look at your past working life. Described below is an activity that I came across while working at IBM. It has proved to be very helpful to coaching clients and team members. Tying this to the Play History activity provides insights that will inform critical elements or ingredients for you to include in your options for more satisfying and meaningful work.

ACTIVITY 5

Job Satisfaction History

Looking back over your work and job history, starting with your most recent role, rate how satisfied you were in each role. Ask yourself "Was the job close to my ideal job? Were the conditions excellent? Was I completely satisfied doing the work?" Rate each of those three components (ideal job, excellent conditions and completely satisfying work) on a scale from 1 (*strongly disagree*) to 7 (*strongly agree*), and then average the total for a final score, or simply think of an overall rating. A score of 7 indicates your ideal job, with excellent conditions and completely satisfying work, whereas 1 indicates the opposite end of the scale. Depending on the extent of your work history, you can detail all of your roles or focus on the last 10 to 15 years. This exercise is informative, but should not be onerous.

Every job is likely to have both positive and negative elements. Write down what was positive and negative for you. Think about the conditions, context and what you were doing. This exercise will provide signals as to the type of activities and work environment you want to move towards and what you want to move away from or minimise.

Table 2: Job Satisfaction History

Job	Satisfaction 1 – 7	Positive	Negative
Manager, Customer Experience	4	• Strong relationships with team and colleagues • Know the job and business well • Close to home and flexible • Reasonable benefits	• My new manager is too hands-on (micromanager) • Lack of freedom and creativity • Lack of challenge and learning • Limited future opportunities
Team Leader, Customer Experience	6	• Collaborative relationship with my manager • Building relationships with team and colleagues • Know the job and business well • Close to home and flexible • Potential for promotion to manager	• Large workload • Income not commensurate with hours and commitment
Team Leader, Customer Service	3	• Opportunity to develop managerial skills • Know the job and business well • Close to home and flexible	• Scope of work very reactive and firefighting only • Majority of time dealing with complaints and angry customers with little scope to rectify their problems • Inexperienced team requires time to build performance
Customer Service Officer	4	• Opportunity to learn new role • Busy role, keeps me challenged • Good ability to balance work and home • Learning about business operations • Some good people to work with	• Some colleagues are very negative and difficult to work with • Company policy leaves little room to rectify customer complaints
Administrator	2	• New industry to learn • Proud to work for this company	• Manager has limited time to help me develop • Limited colleagues to be friendly with

Ratings 1 = Strongly disagree 2 = Disagree 3 = Slightly disagree 4 = Neither agree nor disagree 5 = Slightly agree 6 = Agree 7 = Strongly agree

As a fan of simple and pragmatic, I recommend you create a table. Table 2 provides an example.

Once you have completed your table, look at any themes that seem to be consistently showing up. The above example reflects John's experience, where he found that building relationships with others, the opportunity to develop and learn, flexibility and proximity to home and working well with his manager all contributed positively to his satisfaction. On the other hand, when there was a lack of learning or challenge, when his manager changed and was more hands-on and controlling and when there was a lack of freedom or ability to address issues his dissatisfaction increased.

On completing this exercise for yourself, you should be able to see themes or recognise key contributing factors. It is equally important to be clear on what you do want, as well as what you don't, and this exercise helps you identify that. When finished, go back and compare your results to the Play History activity. Are there any similarities between your early memories of play and your more satisfying jobs? Reflect on the jobs that were more positive and why that was. When did you feel more energised and enthusiastic? What were you doing? If you are someone who likes to learn from visuals, it can be helpful to plot your job satisfaction history in a line graph. See Figure 2 as an example.

Coming back to the washing machine analogy, you can make a change and stop the rinse-and-repeat cycle, but you need to get out of the washing machine in order to do that successfully. Pause, play and rewind are key strategies to help you get clarity on your needs and wants and to minimise or overcome things that might hinder you, such as negative thoughts and responding to potential stressors. Incorporating more opportunities for pause and play in your daily life moving forward will help you perform at your best and contribute positively to your ongoing wellbeing and satisfaction with life in general.

You've now spent some time reflecting on your past to identify some of the necessary ingredients for what you want to move toward. Next, you'll look ahead to build a picture of the future you want, not just for your career but for other priorities in your life.

Figure 2: Job Satisfaction History Visual

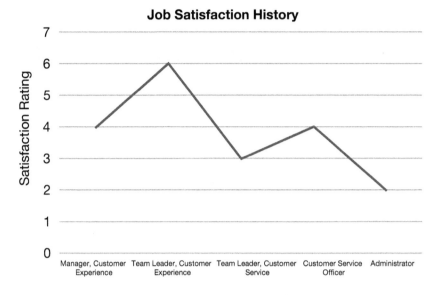

3 THE WHOLE PICTURE

For most people, there is no light from above, no message from God or the universe, no single divine calling. At any age it's ok to still be trying to figure out what you want to be and do with your life. What's important is what you choose to do about it.

Many of us are guilty of comparing ourselves too often to others who seem to have it all. We assume that the outward facade of the storybook picture of success reflects the reality. Having over 20 years of experience in the corporate world, I can share that the saying "looks can be deceiving" certainly has some truth to it. One executive in an organisation I worked for was revered in industry as being a thought leader, progressive and seemingly had it all. He held a powerful C-suite position, had a loving partner, children in private school, a home that looked like it belonged in *Home Beautiful* and a holiday house. Incredibly driven and hardworking, he was recognised as a career success story, a picture of having it all. The reality: date night with his partner needed to be scheduled and it was only through the commitment and determination of his executive assistant that date night happened at all. One of his children had some challenges at school, which caused anxiety, and the compounding nature of his extensive travel for work and late nights in the office heightened the child's anxiety. Eventually, his drive and determination to succeed at all costs contributed to his missing the signals that he had lost support from the CEO and his peers, which meant he'd fail regardless of the effort he put in. While there were many signs that there was something wrong, he persevered nonetheless, until, on getting ready for work one morning, he collapsed and passed out. After a hospital visit and a week of forced bed rest, he returned to work explaining the incident as a pre-existing condition. Within 6 months, however, he had left the organisation, prompted by a serious push from the CEO and board members. It took a while for him to come to terms with the experience, to learn from his mistakes and ultimately reinvent himself and secure a new role that is hopefully a better fit for his strengths and capabilities, and leaves more time and energy to focus on other priorities: his family and his health.

I share this story not to pass judgement (like most of us, he was trying to do his best in what was a challenging context for anyone to succeed) but as a demonstration that there are many facets to a satisfying and meaningful life and your work and career can, and should, be a fulfilling part of the whole. However, when you don't have a clear picture of all of your priorities and what you want them to be, then you are at risk of making decisions in one area that negatively impact more important things.

Work, both paid and unpaid, is an important component of life and influences your life satisfaction. Succeeding at work doesn't happen in isolation of the other parts of life.

Are you clear on what your priorities in life are? Are you clear on what matters most to you? Are you happy and satisfied with your life or are there some things that you have hopes and dreams for? Being aware of your priorities in life and your hopes for the future informs your career choices and increases your chances of greater satisfaction with work; it helps you adapt and make decisions as things happen and life changes.

Perhaps you already intuitively know that a whole-of-person and whole-of-life approach is important, or maybe you've read something similar elsewhere. However, the structure I recommend here is pragmatic, helps you make better career choices and also gives you the confidence to take a risk and pursue the future you hope for.

Additionally, I recommend you refrain from a single label, and instead identify a set of ingredients that you want in work and in life. The activity in this chapter will help you do that by reviewing nine components of life: physical health, relationships, home, emotional wellbeing, career, finances, passions and hobbies, spirituality and community.

Table 3a: Work and Life Priorities

Physical health	Relationships (partner, family, children, close friends)	Home
Emotional wellbeing	Career	Finances
Passions and hobbies	Spirituality	Community

very satisfied	somewhat satisfied	neither satisfied nor dissatisfied	somewhat dissatisfied	very dissatisfied

ACTIVITY 6

Work and Life Priorities

The purpose of this activity is to give you some structure to help you reflect on these priorities as they are for you now, and then how you would like them to be in the future. The activity asks you to think about how satisfied you are with these key components and then build a picture of some broad goals for each component. The activity and components are adapted from the Satisfaction with Life Scale.[1]

There are two parts to this activity.

1. Review Table 3a and think about how satisfied you are with each component. Rate each component choosing from *very satisfied, somewhat satisfied, neither satisfied nor dissatisfied, somewhat dissatisfied* or *very dissatisfied.*

Table 3b: Work and Life Priorities Activity

Physical health	Relationships	Home
• Ideal:	• Ideal:	• Ideal:
• Conditions:	• Conditions:	• Conditions:
• Most important:	• Most important:	• Most important:
• Anything missing:	• Anything missing:	• Anything missing:
• Change:	• Change:	• Change:
Emotional wellbeing	**Career**	**Finances**
• Ideal:	• Ideal:	• Ideal:
• Conditions:	• Conditions:	• Conditions:
• Most important:	• Most important:	• Most important:
• Anything missing:	• Anything missing:	• Anything missing:
• Change:	• Change:	• Change:
Passions and hobbies	**Spirituality**	**Community**
• Ideal:	• Ideal:	• Ideal:
• Conditions:	• Conditions:	• Conditions:
• Most important:	• Most important:	• Most important:
• Anything missing:	• Anything missing:	• Anything missing:
• Change:	• Change:	• Change:
For each component: • What would close to ideal look like? • What conditions would make it excellent? • Do you have what is most important? • If not, what is missing? • Is there anything you would change?		

2. Thinking about each component, write down the answers to the following:

   What would close to ideal look like?

What conditions would make it excellent?

Do you have what is most important?

If not, what is missing?

Is there anything you would change?

Putting pen to paper is important and you can also create a visual representation with a vision board (Pinterest or an old-fashioned corkboard and images).

At this point, while you are still trying to gain clarity, you may want to just write down a couple of sentences, answering the above questions and describing both how it could look and feel. If you want to vary the components, feel free to categorise different areas in your life in any way that makes sense to you.

When you are describing your ideal, effectively you are starting to form goals. Be sure to focus on what you can control and influence. For example, you can't control someone else's happiness but you can work towards having a supportive and heathy relationship with that person.

A few pointers for each:

Physical health – If you are happy with your physical health then simply maintaining your existing health is great. Most of us would like to improve some area of our physical health. You might be thinking, how is this relevant to planning for the career I want? But as you make your way through the chapters, activities and stories, hopefully you'll see how interconnected everything is. For example, a job that is close to home might make it easier for you to get to the gym before or after work, which will mean that you're physically fit and capable to perform at your best and/or meet the physical demands of your work.

Relationships – Significant research and evidence exists to support the concept that "other people matter."[2] Having, maintaining and developing healthy positive relationships brings about significant benefits, such as overall wellbeing, feelings of happiness, sense of security, belonging and self-worth.[3] For the purposes of this activity, focus on your closest relationships.

Home – Your home, or where you live, provides you with one of your fundamental human needs for safety. It may or may not be a priority for you to change anything about your home at the moment, but the place and space in which you rest and live will have an impact on the other components of your life. Write down what you want from your home, how it makes you feel and what activities it enables you to do because of the space it provides.

Emotional wellbeing – Emotional wellbeing is about how you feel, how often you experience positive emotions like joy, love and compassion, and healthy psychological functioning. Emotions change and don't remain in a fixed and permanent state. While I'm a highly optimistic person, I don't promote a "Pollyanna," rose-coloured glasses, "wish and ye shall receive" approach, but rather a focus on progress and making things better for people. The beauty of the interconnectedness of wellbeing is that focusing on some of the other components, such as relationships or physical health, will have an upward spiral effect on your emotional wellbeing.[4]

Career – Assuming that you're reading this book because you want to gain greater satisfaction from your work, this expands further on the Job Satisfaction History activity. For this exercise, there is no need to include a specific job title. Instead describe what you want from your work, and how you want it to look, feel and fit in with/enable the rest of your life. Regardless of whether you view work as a job, a career or a calling, everyone deserves to be and feel valued for the work they do and to gain satisfaction from their time spent contributing to work. Work can provide many benefits outside of financial necessity, such as opportunities to learn, build relationships, experience enjoyment, feel a sense of achievement and belonging, and contribute to something greater. What do you want work to be and do for you?

Finances – What financial resources would you ideally like to have? Research shows that the lack of basic resources and materials (such as income) does contribute to unhappiness; however, an increase in these resources does not increase happiness. Maybe you've personally experienced this: a great-paying job that initially provided a sense of worth and satisfaction from the attached dollar figure, but the satisfaction was short-lived once you became accustomed to the income, and the work or demands of the job remained unsatisfying.

If you are in the situation where your lack of financial resources is contributing to significant concerns for you, please don't let that stop you pursuing satisfying and meaningful work. It might be that you have to take a job that is a stopgap to address this need, but you can still set a goal and work on a plan to move onto something better. Sandy's story, in Part Three, demonstrates an example of this.

A trustworthy financial planner can help you achieve longer-term financial goals. Alternatively, there are a number of great resources available. In Australia, moneysmart.gov.au is a government-backed initiative to empower people to be in control of their financial lives through providing free tools, tips and guidance. There are also a number of helpful books, such as Scott Pape's best-selling *The Barefoot Investor*.

Passions and hobbies – This is where you have opportunities for leisure and play. These are activities that have the characteristics of play mentioned in Chapter 2: you choose to do it, you make your own decisions, you enjoy the process, there are both rules and room for creativity, and it is imaginative and conducted in an active, but relatively non-stressed frame of mind. Are there hobbies or interests that you used to make time for and thoroughly enjoyed, but for some reason you've stopped? Or are there activities you've always wanted to try, but have not made time for?

Spirituality – "Come on lady, you're losing me here!" Agnostic, atheist, religious, pagan or spiritual by your own definition: if formalised religion is a priority for you then this will be clear. For others, being in nature similarly fulfils this role: a sense of belonging, a safe space, an opportunity to clear your mind and for inner harmony. Perhaps think about the activities that you would describe as good for your soul.

Community – We all live in a community and you may already actively support and engage in your community through volunteering or local sporting or hobby clubs. For some this may not be something that you've historically prioritised or actively participated in. Volunteering and involvement in community organisations return benefits to you personally, to the others you interact with and to the wider community as well as the opportunity to contribute to something greater. The impact of the health crisis has brought communities together and this focus on greater connection to your local community is something that will likely increase in importance for many people.

Overall, this activity can take a little time and is something you might come back to again. As you progress through the activities in later chapters, you may decide to change what you want from these components. Personally, I complete this activity in my journal every year, helping to set my goals for the year ahead.

Throughout the book, you'll focus on further expanding on what improving satisfaction from your work means for you: the necessary ingredients. And as part of that, it's important to consider how all the components connect and impact one another and how, at various stages of life, some components will be more of a priority or impact the decisions and actions taken in others.

You may have come across similar activities, defining life domains, components or factors in other books or resources. With human history as it exists, there is not much that is completely new: most things are built from the work that has gone before. View this and the following activities as a way to be of most help to you, by combining and adapting a range of theories, models and frameworks in a way that is practical, pragmatic and helpful. If you want to dig deeper into any of the topics, feel free to explore the cited resources included at the back for ease of reading.

"Action expresses priorities."

Mahatma Gandhi

To help you improve or change your work, you're now clearer on how career fits with the rest of how you want your life to be. It's not practical to change every component of your life at the one time, especially if you are setting ambitious goals that require significant change. While all of these components in life matter to you, you need to prioritise which you will action first or sooner. And while work is one of those components, you may choose one or two other components to help improve your overall satisfaction with life. But how do you choose? Well, the good news is you already have an inbuilt system that helps you make decisions; you just might not be consciously aware of what that system is for you. Understanding your values uncovers your inbuilt decision-making system, as discussed in the next chapter.

4 DRIVING DECISIONS

In order to build a plan to find and create more meaningful work, it's important to be clear on what drives your decisions. Your values are formed from a young age, and unconsciously inform your inbuilt decision-making system.

Do you notice history repeating itself when you look back on your career? Have you found yourself in similar but different situations and wondered, how did I get here again? Or have you found yourself stuck, unable to move forward and make a change even though you know definitively that you want to?

One of my clients Sam found himself in his 11th year in an organisation that specialised in retail architecture. He loved the work that he did and had great relationships with his clients. However, the owner of the firm had a high need for control, demonstrated a lack of trust with staff and was not supportive of flexible working. When I met with Sam, he was conflicted. Even though he knew the working environment could be so much better and he definitely wanted to make a change, something was holding him back. He'd moved from Scotland to be with his beautiful and supportive Australian wife, now raising two children whom they adore. His wife encouraged him to make a change and suggested that he and I work together to prepare for that change. She felt that his low tolerance for risk was holding him back. In a way she was right;

however, it was through completing a values activity that Sam could understand what was driving his internal conflict and subsequent lack of action.

Every person holds a set of values that are guiding principles of what is most important to them in life. Mostly you will find that your values are unconsciously driving your decisions daily, as part of your inbuilt decision-making system. What is helpful with values is not that you have them (because everybody does), but the priority order of importance that you place on them and that they are critical motivators of behaviour.[1] When something causes a conflict between two or more values that are important to you, you'll begin to notice your priority values as you evaluate, judge and decide on a course of action.

Sam completed the activity that you will find below, and identified that family and financial security were in his top five as being most important to him. The situation he found himself in at work had these two values in conflict. The lack of flexibility actually ate away at his value of family in little ways every day, when he would leave the office at 5pm under glaring scrutiny, despite the fact that he was the first person to arrive in the morning. Living regionally, getting home in time to share the evening meal was precious family time. Yet, holding him in the job was the priority importance he placed on financial security. He realised that his upbringing in Scotland was probably the genesis for this value. He was able to understand his value of financial security not as a negative, but as something that he needed to satisfy in order to make a change. Working with his values, rather than against, we set a strategy of securing a job else-where first, and confirming that it aligned to his values before he made any decision as to the best approach for him. It is unlikely that we would have agreed on any other strategy, but simply being aware and conscious of his values and how he could satisfy them helped him make a decision to start taking action and prepare to explore career opportunities. Sam was approached by an organisation doing similar work, but offering more leadership responsibilities, greater growth and significant flexibility. Because he had been through the values activity and was clear on what he wanted from his next role (plus having an amazing resumé), he was well prepared to capitalise on this opportunity that presented itself. When I last checked in with him, he was thoroughly enjoying his new role and was very pleased he had made the decision to make a change.

You have just spent time reviewing different parts of your life and in each component, outlining what is important to you. Of course, there is a strong overlap between that activity and understanding your values. The difference is that your values are part of your inbuilt decision-making system. They help you evaluate, judge and make decisions in order to take action. If you look at some of the components of life, yes, they are all important but at different stages of your life you will prioritise what you do about them and when. As an example, sleep is critical for your physical health; however, if you have ever taken care of a newborn baby, you will have experienced that it is not something you can prioritise over meeting your baby's needs.

There's no definitive list of values. Various programs offer lists most commonly used in this type of activity and an internet search will bring up a multitude of these and a range of experts in their fields who incorporate values into their work and research, such as Brené Brown[2] and many others.

You can describe and label values in whatever way has meaning for you. And many can have similar meanings but be labelled differently by different people. For example, one person may value fairness and describe the meaning for them as what you do for one person, you do for many; whereas another would describe equality and treating people equally. What's important is that it resonates for you. Review Table 4 for a list of values arranged under the components of life.

Research has shown that like our human need for play, values have been proven to be cross-cultural; however, in both play and values, your culture will impact the importance of certain values and different types of play. Sam's story demonstrates how understanding both what you want your life to be and the values that drive your decisions can help you more effectively pursue your goals.

Table 4: Values and Components of Life

Physical health	Relationships (partner, family, children, close friends)	Home
Adventure, Achievement, Challenge, Competence, Leadership	Family, Fun, Friendship, Love, Loyalty, Honesty, Respect, Trustworthiness, Social connection, Responsibility	Security, Belonging, Stability, Beauty

Emotional wellbeing	Career	Finances
Authenticity, Balance, Integrity, Openness, Optimism, Inner harmony, Self-respect	Achievement, Authority, Belonging, Creativity, Curiosity, Challenge, Contribution, Equity, Inclusion, Knowledge, Leadership, Learning, Reputation, Wisdom	Security, Responsibility, Stability, Status, Success, Wealth

Passions and hobbies	Spirituality	Community
Beauty, Belonging, Bravery, Creativity, Curiosity, Determination, Excellence, Fun, Freedom, Learning, Social connection	Faith, Inner harmony, Meaning, Unity with nature, Loyalty, Peace	Beauty, Citizenship, Compassion, Contribution, Generosity, Kindness, Fairness, Friendship, Learning, Reputation, Service

ACTIVITY 7

Your Priority Values

Grab a piece of paper, some Post-It notes and a pen. I recommend choosing someone who you trust to do this activity with: a friend or partner.

First, identify a long list of your values. Review Table 4 for inspiration.

Write down what you value most.

Once you have a long list, think about the last difficult decision you made. What were the underlying values that helped you make your final decision or judgement? Add these if you had not thought of them already and asterisk them.

Next look at your "hot buttons." Think about the last time something really made you angry. It was likely that something conflicted with or went against one of your values. Again, add them if they are not already written down and asterisk them.

The aim of this activity is to choose five values that are most important. This is the hard part, because they are all important. And yes, five is an arbitrary number; you could choose six or more, but from a pragmatic point of view, five makes it manageable and easier to inform your career or job choices.

Write the five priority values on separate Post-It notes.

This is where it is helpful to talk through the activity with someone else. Take any two of the five and imagine you are faced with a situation that forced you choose one value; that is, the situation meant two values conflicted and you could not honour both. For example, you have a value of freedom and you also have a priority value of family and you often find that you prioritise your family over your own freedom.

Explain each value to your partner or friend, including what it means to you, and describe if a situation or event forced you to prioritise one value over the other, what would come first. Then place the two Post-It notes down in order of priority.

Select another Post-It note and compare that value to the two you just discussed. Again, talk through a comparison of the value to each one. What order of priority would it take now? Continue until you have your list of priority values in order from one to five.

If you are doing this with your significant other, you might find that the value priorities explain some of the disagreements that regularly appear in your relationship. For example, your partner might value achievement, and therefore focuses on getting things done, whereas you value excellence, and can get frustrated that things are not finished to a high standard.

It is important to do this activity without judgement. Try not to compare your priorities in a way that passes negative judgement. But do discuss them, and reflect on how these values may have impacted previous decisions or actions in your work choices. Have they been helpful, or perhaps are they leading to choices and decisions that have proved not to be very satisfying or enjoyable?

By working with, rather than against, your values, your chances of success and achieving satisfying work are greater. For example, if you have a priority value of challenge, it indicates that you are likely to want to secure a role that provides you with new challenges, rather than more of what you have already done. It means you may compromise something else that you value to achieve it; perhaps in this case financial security is a lower priority, so you are prepared to take a lower salary initially to experience a greater challenge in a new industry. Or it may mean that your value of belonging is holding you back from taking action, as you have such strong relationships and a sense of belonging where you are that you stay even though the work itself is no longer interesting or providing any opportunities to learn. If you think some of your values prevent you from taking action, talk this through as part of the activity.

In your journal, write down the five values in priority order and any insights on how your priority values have or are impacting your choices for the work that you do.

It can get confusing because the same term can refer to both a value and a trait, for example "curiosity," "fun" or "creativity." According to one of the leading researchers on values, "Traits are tendencies to show consistent patterns of thought, feelings, and actions across time and situations. ... They describe what you are like rather than what you consider important."[3]

Values are an important part of your personality and who you are, but the critical distinction is that they motivate behaviours and attitudes: they are part of your inbuilt decision-making system and the reason you do what you do. Being clear on your priority values will help you pursue and assess options for your career or next job that give you the greatest chance for satisfaction and success. As an added bonus, it might even help you avoid arguments or understand why others behave the way they do.

As values drive decisions that motivate us to act, we're going to next look at your experiences at work and when you have enjoyed what you are doing most and why, to further inform your necessary ingredients for satisfying work.

5 FLOW

Hopefully, you have had experiences in both work and play where you have found yourself so involved in the activity that nothing else seemed to matter; the experience so enjoyable that you did it for the sheer sake of it. This is what is known as a state of flow. The Play and Job Satisfaction History activities both identified activities you enjoyed most and in what context, pointing to times when you're likely to have experienced this state of flow. The concept comes from years of research by psychologist Mihaly Csikszentmihalyi on what people most enjoy doing and why.

Regularly experiencing a state of flow during your work and other activities provides for greater satisfaction and happiness in life. Csikszentmihalyi is well known for his research and best-selling book, *Flow: The Psychology of Optimal Experience* (1990) in which he states that happiness "is a condition that must be prepared for, cultivated and defended by each person. People who learn to control their inner experience will be able to determine the quality of their lives, which is as close as any of us can become to being happy."[1] He describes how optimal experiences can add up to "a sense of participation in determining the content of life." Through his research, he explored how people felt when they most enjoyed themselves and why. Studies showed that regardless of culture, age or gender, people universally described the optimal experience in the same way. The concept of "flow is the state in which people are so involved in an activity that nothing else seems to matter; the experience so enjoyable that people will do it for the sheer sake of it, even at great cost."[2]

Integral to the concept of flow is recognising that everything we experience is represented in the mind as information: data if you will. We are able to respond to this information and decide what our lives will be like and take action to pursue that.

Let me provide a very broad range of examples that you can perhaps relate to. A merchandiser working in retail so enjoys putting displays together that she doesn't notice the time passing, and would almost do the work for free. Many jobs, especially in the corporate world, involve the creation of PowerPoint presentations. The task on its own may seem mundane, but for many, their interest in the subject matter and the opportunity to create and communicate something powerful, helpful and meaningful for others renders the experience enjoyable; it involves some challenge and requires enough focus that time can pass unnoticed. Maybe you've experienced the state of flow in brain-storming activities with colleagues where you are dreaming up a new product or solving a problem. Others might experience the state of flow in activities working more on their own, such as writing or editing communications for a business or program, developing websites or editing videos. There are many different activities that can provide opportunities for a state of flow during work.

Exploring when you have experienced flow before will help you continue to build and clarify the list of necessary ingredients for satis-fying and meaningful work. When you secure work that gives you more opportunities to experience a state of flow, you will increase your sense of enjoyment and satisfaction and provide for greater meaning.

To recognise the experience of flow, look for activities where:

- The activity is challenging and requires some skill
- Your attention is focused, and you have full concentration on what you are doing
- The activity has clear goals
- You know instantly how you are doing (immediate feedback)

- You're not worried about failure
- Self-consciousness disappears
- You lose track of time
- The experience of the activity is its own reward.

For some it could be the experience of facilitating a meeting. I see you rolling your eyes into the back of your head. Yes, admittedly, meetings can be one of the most painful experiences in the workplace. However, there is real skill in facilitating effective meetings. Someone with these skills, or a trained facilitator, will find for them that they are fully focused and concentrating on what they are doing, their goal is to achieve a key outcome from the meeting, they immediately know how they are doing from observing and engaging with participants, they aren't self-conscious and although keeping to time is part of the objective, the experience of time goes very quickly; what takes an hour or more seems much shorter. The experience itself is the main reward; there is satisfaction in the achievement in itself, even though it is a requirement of their job and what they are paid to do. Facilitating a group of people to achieve an agreed outcome through discussion requires skill and also provides a challenge.

Maybe you've noticed this need for the right amount of challenge in your own experience at work. When there is a lack of challenge and your skills are not utilised, work can be boring. When a task is too difficult or ambiguous, or requires too many skills that you don't have, work can be stressful or frustrating.

ACTIVITY 8

Your Experiences of Flow

In your journal, write down your most recent experience where you were in a state of flow in the work you were doing; that is, so involved in the activity that nothing else seemed to matter, you enjoyed the sheer act of doing it and you lost track of time.

Capture:

- What you were doing

- The conditions and environment

- How challenging it was

- The skills you were using.

Review your Job Satisfaction History activity and your most satisfying roles. Were there more opportunities where you experienced a state of flow in these jobs? If so, why? Use Table 5 as a template to start building a list of what you need for more enjoyment in the work you do now and also in what is next for you.

Table 5: My Experiences of Flow at Work

Activity / Work	Conditions and Environment	Level of Challenge (low, medium, high)	Skills Used

Understanding your experiences of the state of flow helps you identify future activities, conditions and environments where you are likely to experience flow more often, which will then lead to more enjoyment and satisfaction.

The skills that you put to use during these flow experiences can also highlight some of your greatest strengths. As shown in the next chapter, through better articulating and leveraging your strengths, you will give yourself the greatest opportunity for successful change.

6 STRENGTHS

You may be familiar with the idea of individual "strengths" and how they are understood in relation to the job application process. Perhaps you have an intuitive idea about what your personal strengths are. Maybe you have done some form of career development before or been through an interview process where you were asked to talk about your strengths. Most people don't feel super comfortable telling others about how great they are. Few of us are comfortable weaving statements such as "What's so special about me is. . ." into everyday conversation. And if you think about it, you've probably experienced similar moments of awkwardness from a young age. Memories of school sports teams and being picked or not. Whispers of "pick her because she is a fast runner, pick him because he is tall" or what's worse is "don't pick them, they are rubbish at this game." However, when you want to make a change to your career or job, it's important to know how to describe your strengths.

We get a little more sophisticated as we get older and enter the world of work, but the career and job-change process can evoke similar feelings of discomfort. With some understanding of the career-change process, you can decide on the best way to communicate to others what you have to offer through the articulation of your strengths.

There are a number of academic definitions of "strengths" that have their roots in traits personality theory. To provide a simple definition, a strength is something you are good at, it energises you and you are drawn to activities that use it.[1] It describes the best of who you are, your personality, your character traits. As mentioned in Chapter 4, traits are "tendencies to show consistent patterns of thought, feelings, and actions across time and situations. . . . They describe what you are like."[2]

Understanding your strengths is a vital ingredient for identifying and planning for more satisfying work; it also gives you the best chance of making a successful change. It's important to have the right language to describe what's unique about you and the value you add to those around you and the work you do. Some examples of strengths are: creativity, curiosity, leadership, teamwork, perseverance and social intelligence.

These terms may seem a little like jargon, but they provide a common language that is understood by many. For example, you might know yourself to be friendly, likeable and even popular; that can translate into strengths for your career as strong relationship-building or customer-focused skills. Maybe you prefer and work best alone; this could be described as the ability to work independently or as self-motivation. Perhaps you are a voracious reader or listener of podcasts; this indicates a love of learning or curiosity.

According to psychologists Chris Peterson and Martin Seligman, in their book *Character Strengths and Virtues*, strengths "focus on what is right about people that make the good life possible."[3] Research has substantiated a number of personal benefits for people who use their strengths regularly. For example, they experience more:

- Happiness
- Confidence
- Energy and vitality
- Resilience
- Work performance and achievement
- Engagement and enjoyment from their work
- Goal achievement
- Personal development.

As humans, we have a survival tendency towards the negative, the potential risks and solving critical ailments. However, the neuroscience research supports that a focus on what is right with people rather than the deficit approach of focusing on what's not provides for greater benefits. As this applies to strengths, it does not promote ignoring weaknesses, but, as the evidence suggests, we are happier, perform better and learn more effectively if we are using and developing more of our strengths. Personally, I am not a huge fan of the term "weakness," perhaps because the definition also applies to ill health and being weak. However, if you consider the word in this context for work, it is the opposite of a strength; therefore, it's something that you are not naturally good at, drains the life out of you and you might avoid doing. "Tell us about your weaknesses" is still a commonly asked question as part of the job-interview process. And while I don't like the term, it is important to understand and acknowledge that there may be gaps in your knowledge, ability and proficiency that will relate to a new role. We'll cover more on understanding and reframing your weaknesses as part of Chapter 8, "Growth."

Much has been studied on strengths since the concept was first popularised in 1999 by Marcus Buckingham and Curt Coffman. In reality, you might not use your strengths in everything you do from a work perspective (or in general for that matter). It's also important to recognise when and where certain strengths are appropriate, depending on the context. For example, a sense of humour is a strength; however, there are situations where you'd choose not to demonstrate or use this strength.

The identification and development of your strengths has many personal benefits, as well as the very practical application for identifying a range of career and job options that you might not have previously considered. From a tactical perspective, it's helpful for your resumé or biography. Many of the exercises included in this book are not a "once-and-done" activity. You'll hopefully continue to build on them, incorporate them into your goals and action plan and they will help you answer interview questions, or inform networking discussions.

There are two broad ways that you can identify your strengths: either through a formal online tool or through a variety of activities. The Flow and Play activities will have pointed to some of your strengths. Everyone has strengths that are valuable and that describe them at their best. The intention here is to help you identify your strengths yourself, in a way that is practical, accessible and easy to understand.

Think about your conversation download at the end of the day. What are you describing when you find yourself talking excitedly? You might notice you talk faster, you're more animated, the pitch of your voice changes and the expression on your face is one of joy or excitement. When this happens for you, what are you describing? What activity are you talking about? What skills are you using and in what context?

Something to watch out for is that your behaviour and excitement levels are a deviation from your usual demeanour. There should be a noticeable positive increase. Some people are very calm and more private. If this sounds like you, then it may just be a small increase in the way you positively describe the work you enjoy doing or would enjoy that indicates a strength.

ACTIVITY 9

Your Strengths

Talk to the people who know you and that you trust, both in and outside of work. Ask them what strengths they value in you – that is, the things you are good at, that seem to energise you – and ask for when they have seen you use them and in what context. Think about any feedback you have received from your manager, colleagues or customers. Even informal positive comments can point to strengths others value in you. For example, "Thanks for turning that piece of work around so quickly" can point to being responsive and efficient.

For some people asking others about your strengths can be an uncomfortable activity. The reason it is valuable is that it's likely you underestimate your abilities, or you view what you do in the context of "anyone would do that in the same situation," and therefore you believe that it is not special or unique. For example, I completed a similar exercise and a close friend commented that she saw "asking for help" as a strength. While I know this about myself, I'd never viewed this as a strength. Yet, imagine a work context if someone were stuck and at a loss for how to solve a problem or move a project forward. You'd expect them to ask for help rather than ruminate and spin their wheels for a long period of time unnecessarily.

One possible approach is contacting people personally and then sending them an email with the definition, providing them time to respond. Include a date for when you would like to receive the feedback and don't expect that everyone will respond. While everyone usually has the best intentions, sometimes they just don't get to it. Once you receive the responses it is helpful to record them and compare the similarities. Ideally, aim for a good cross-section of friends, family and trusted work colleagues; six or more responses will give you a good reference point.

ONLINE TOOLS

A widely used free tool is the VIA Survey, created from the work of Chris Peterson and Martin Seligman, which classifies 24 character strengths that have been tested across cultures and are universally recognised as good. The survey is free, quick and simple and you can access it from https://www.viacharacter.org. When you receive your results, you may find that some of the strengths included don't seem to fit in the context of work, such as "capacity to love and be loved," "gratitude" and "appreciation of beauty and excellence." Capacity to love and be loved points to close relationships; would you say that you value and are able to build good relationships with those at work? Do you have genuine concern for the welfare of your teammates, colleagues or the people you manage? Then perhaps this is how this strength shows up for you in the context of your career and work.

Gratitude is about expressing your thanks. Think about how this might show up at work. Again, it might point to an ability to build relationships or engender trust. For those who appreciate beauty and excellence, in a work setting this might show up in attention to detail or ensuring presentations are always professional and designed specifically for the optimal user experience. Now these are not traits, or strengths in this academic context, but they are very useful learnt and developed skills in a work context.

Like most of the topics covered in this section, strengths don't work in isolation of your life and experiences. Context and significant life events can shape your strengths and change them over time. Therefore, you might consider repeating the survey from time to time.

Many of the stories included in Part Three illustrate the power of understanding your strengths and then being able to articulate them. When looking for a more satisfying career, or simply to enjoy your day-to-day work more, your strengths are a key ingredient and using them regularly increases happiness, performance, energy and vitality.

Your strengths describe what you are like, and when it comes to your work, future employers will want to know that. They will also want to know what you are capable of; that is, what you can do. The next chapter will address the importance of understanding your capabilities: a combination of your skills and your knowledge.

7 CAPABILITIES

As part of making any career change or job move, you need to be able to articulate what you are like and what you are capable of, both your strengths and your capabilities. Many people struggle with identifying their capabilities – that is, their skills and knowledge. There are a few reasons for this; one is that we often don't consciously think about the skills and knowledge we use to do things. Like driving a car, once the skills are learnt they become automatic. The other is that it can be coloured by the view you have of yourself. What you may think is common, or something everyone does easily, may not be the case. You may also not realise what other people value or need help with.

One of my clients came to me lamenting that she had a fairly incoherent career trajectory. When we talked through the very varied jobs that she'd had, there was a common theme of communication. What she was great at, and enjoyed doing, was written communication, through a vast array of channels and industries. So much so, that she did this in her own time with a passion project of writing a book and volunteering on the board for a writer's festival. With the help of clarifying her reasons for doing what she did, her "why," and being able to understand her skills, knowledge and experience in this light, she successfully changed her career from media and communications in a not-for-profit organisation to a learning/information design manager working with clients in the financial services sector.

Perhaps you can relate to a career where you feel like you have randomly moved from one thing to another. However, there will be some consistency in how you have used both your strengths and capabilities; and you probably will have been drawn to work that uses them in some way.

The Job Satisfaction History activity should have identified some of your capabilities. A comprehensive list of capabilities would fill this book; however, some common examples are: project management, written and verbal communication, budget management, event coordination, building relationships, customer focus, design, and risk management.

I've worked with people who have been in the one company all their working life, as well as mothers returning to the workforce after many years at home. I've noticed that we tend to underestimate our capabilities, or forget that in our personal life we use our capabilities every day.

A friend of mine trained and worked as a primary school teacher and then chose to be a stay-at-home mum to raise her four children. Her teaching skills certainly came in handy while home-schooling four children during two long COVID-19 lockdowns. She is working towards combining her passion for psychology and philosophy into a business of her own, after she completes her master's in positive psychology. While she has not been in paid work for over 10 years, she has continued to develop her skills and knowledge. Being president of the school board has honed her decision-making, collaboration, persuasion and influencing skills. She has an amazing ability to comprehend and recall science and research and her written and verbal communication skills are also very strong. Juggling the family responsibilities of four children, and a husband who has travelled a lot for work, means that even without necessarily realising it, she is very efficient at juggling competing demands, negotiating and finding a compromise, and is hardworking, which almost goes without saying (but you must say it!). Using all of these skills and knowledge will give her the best chance of building a successful business.

ACTIVITY 10

Your Capabilities

This activity is based on a worksheet I created. It helps you identify your capabilities and understand how to best use them through a number of steps.

First, reflect on the past 12 months and in your journal, or on a piece of paper, write down the key things or projects you worked on or participated in, big or small; include unpaid work, any volunteering, events or activities you contributed to or participated in, such as fund-raising, social events, coaching sporting teams, school activities, even social networking. Once you have your list, circle a couple that you are most proud of.

Reflect on this work and identify the capabilities that you applied. Remember, capabilities include your people and technical skills and knowledge.

If you need inspiration, search the internet for position descriptions or job advertisements for similar roles to the work you identified. Look at the required skills and knowledge they are asking for. If you work in a field that has a professional association, their website may also have some helpful materials.

I recommend keeping to generic terms, generally one or two words, and often a verb for a skill. This is because once completed, this activity will help you with your resumé and interviewing. Specialist skills or knowledge may sometimes be three word – for example, creative design solutions, human-centred design, power system design or public event management. Don't forget to list both people and technical skills; for example, communication and building relationships are people skills that are often critical for success.

An example is provided below of someone who currently performs a business manager role, having taken on a role in the infrastructure industry in the last few years.

Table 6: Example Capabilities List – Business Manager

People Skills	Technical Skills	Knowledge
Leadership	Sales forecasting	Financial and budgetary processes
Coaching	Managing employees and resources	Infrastructure industry
Developing others	Productivity growth/ improvement	Safety
Performance management	Problem-solving	
Written and verbal communication	Managing profit and loss	
Building partner relationships	Competitor analysis	
	Business strategy	
	Microsoft Office suite	

If you are finding this challenging, ask a colleague or someone you trust to talk it through. Sometimes, just discussing it with someone helps you articulate your skills and knowledge more effectively.

Once you have listed the capabilities that you've applied to work or other activities, review the list and select the 10 most complex or challenging and write them down. Ensure a mix of all three types: technical skills, people skills and knowledge. Review each of these capabilities, assessing your level of interest and how proficient you believe you are. Refer to the template in Table 7a to complete your assessment.

This step provides valuable data about your skills and knowledge. Reviewing how interested you are in a particular capability points to whether this is something you want more of or less of in your next role. Adding how proficient you are helps identify your best capabilities to leverage for a change, and also what would be best for you to develop.

Table 7a: Top 10 Capabilities

Capability	Interest	Proficiency
1.		
2.		
3.		
4.		
5.		
6.		
7.		
8.		
9.		
10.		

Level of interest:
1. Very uninterested   2. Uninterested   3. Neutral   4. Interested   5. Very Interested
Level of proficiency:
1. Needs significant improvement   2. Needs some development   3. Capable
4. Highly capable and effective   5. Role model/expert

The example of the business manager can help bring this to life (refer to Table 7b).

Table 7b: Example: Top 10 Capabilities for Business Manager

Capability	Interest	Proficiency
1. Leadership	5	4
2. Building partner relationships	4	4
3. Developing others	4	3
4. Managing profit and loss	3	4
5. Productivity growth/improvement	2	4
6. Business strategy	3	4
7. Sales forecasting	2	3
8. Financial and budgetary processes	3	3
9. Safety	4	2
10. Infrastructure industry	2	2

Level of interest:
1. Very uninterested   2. Uninterested   3. Neutral   4. Interested   5. Very Interested

Level of proficiency:
1. Needs significant improvement   2. Needs some development   3. Capable
4. Highly capable and effective   5. Role model/expert

Plotting these results on a grid will help you visually understand these capabilities. Refer to Table 8a for the template and Table 8b for the business manager example.

Table 8a: Plotting Your Capabilities

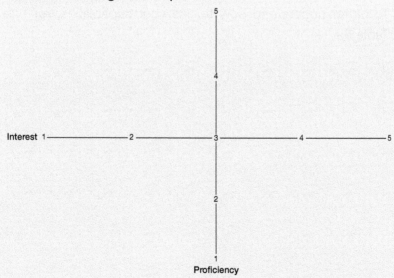

53

Table 8b: Example: Plotting Capabilities Business Manager

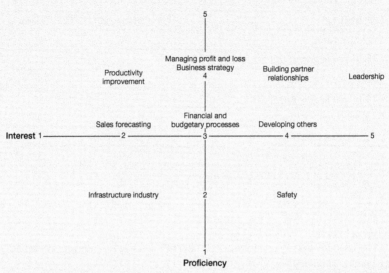

Plot your capabilities in the grid. Do they paint an accurate picture of the value you bring? If you feel it is lacking, add another three to five capabilities. Also include capabilities from your hobbies or interests outside of work that best reflect what you enjoy doing.

To better understand how to use your capabilities, refer to Table 9a.

Table 9a: How Best to Use Your Capabilities

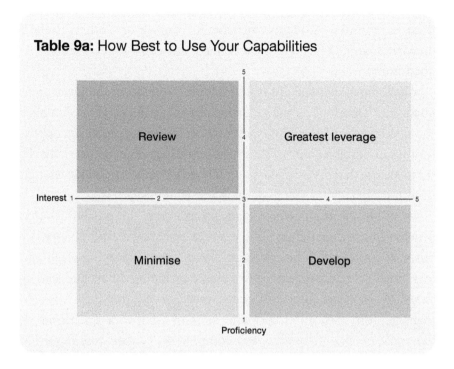

Capabilities in the top left quadrant, "Review," are capabilities you are good at, but in which you have low interest. There are parts of all work that we don't enjoy but they're necessary. If a large number of your capabilities fall in this quadrant, it would be worth exploring what would bring more joy into your work and probably confirms that it is time for a change.

Capabilities in the bottom left quadrant, "Minimise," help you identify activities or job requirements that would be best to minimise or avoid. If you spend a lot of your current time using these capabilities it is unlikely to be satisfying or sustainable. Look for opportunities to delegate or outsource if possible. In planning for future work, ensure the next job does not require using these a lot.

Your capabilities with the "Greatest leverage" to make a change will fall in the top right quadrant, as they capture what you are good at and interested in. This includes anything that falls on the axis at or above a 3 for both interest and proficiency. Leveraging these to make a change will set you up best for success. Also think about sharing this expertise by helping others to improve these capabilities. Continuing to improve these capabilities will deliver benefits to yourself and others. Reflect on what it would take to be even better at any capabilities listed in this quadrant.

Capabilities that you are still developing will fall in the lower right quadrant, "Develop," as you are interested in and enjoy them, but have room to improve. In looking to make a change, ensure there are opportunities to develop some of these as part of that change. Alternatively, try to ensure that the next work you pursue will at least provide enough time and capacity for you to develop these interests.

If we look at the business manager example, the capabilities that provide them with the greatest leverage for a successful change are business strategy, building partner relationships, managing profit and loss, financial and budgetary processes, developing others and leadership. These are the core skills and knowledge required for a business manager role, indicating they like most of what they do. However, like most people, there are a few components of their role requiring skills and knowledge where they are capable, but there is no longer much interest (sales forecasting and productivity improvement). The infrastructure industry is not something they know a lot about, only having been in that industry for a couple of years, but it appears they have found that the industry lacks the appeal they thought they would find. One benefit of working in infrastructure is that it does provide the opportunity to develop safety knowledge, which is something they are interested in improving and building.

There are a number of steps to this activity, so if you are not used to completing these types of worksheets, you might benefit from doing the exercise a second time, once you understand how it comes together.

The Your Capabilities activity is great to share in a team setting as it can give you a view of the capabilities that exist within a team, and these are best leveraged to explore growth, innovation or problem-solving in any business.

You have a vast array of capabilities, more than the 10 or so that you've included here. This simply provides a good starting point regarding the careers or jobs your capabilities are best transferred to

Table 9b: Example: Business Manager Capabilities

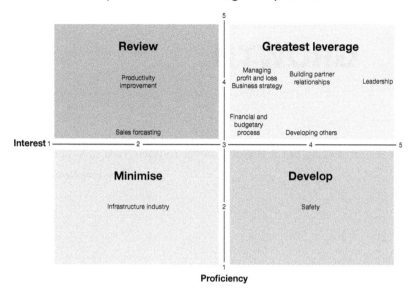

and how to articulate what you are capable of. When you combine your strengths with your capabilities and you have a clear understanding of them, you are ready to answer those questions that will no doubt be a part of your journey ahead: "Tell us about yourself?" and "What are your strengths and areas for development?" Or, if you create your own business, "What makes you unique?" and "Why should I buy from you?"

Now that you are forming this picture of yourself that incorporates your values, strengths and capabilities, hopefully your confidence is growing in regards to tackling the career-change process. It should also start to become clearer how your unique combination of skills and knowledge can be applied to a range of jobs or careers.

Making any form of change requires openness and adaptability, and the next chapter looks at growth and the mindset needed to enable it.

8 GROWTH

"It is hard to fail, but it is worse never to have tried to succeed."

Theodore Roosevelt

A focus on continual growth and learning in your career and life is important. And it's likely you know through experience that life and work are not success-only journeys. There are challenges, failures, successes, high and low points. The reflection activities you have completed so far confirm that you have a desire to change, that you have hopes for a different future and that you have strengths and capabilities. There's a yearning for greater fulfilment, to explore what's possible and to do and be more. You've gathered a picture of what can help you; but the picture is not complete without growth, and a key part of growth is learning from failure, your attitude towards challenges and your beliefs about yourself.

In facing the change journey ahead, do you hold any beliefs or attitudes such as "I am no good at interviews," "I'm not a good public speaker," "I'm not great at selling myself" or "I'm not good at using LinkedIn to network"? Or is the mere thought of applying for jobs and putting yourself out there so daunting that it is safer not to try?

You may have heard or know a bit about mindset already. Mindset is a set of beliefs or way of thinking that determines one's behaviour, outlook and mental attitude. Frances's story in Part Three demonstrates a growth mindset in many ways: her focus on continual learning, her embracing of challenges and opportunities and her perseverance through difficult times.

You might be familiar with the vacuum brand Dyson, but you might not know that James Dyson was so frustrated with his family's vacuum cleaner that he invented and tested over 5000 prototypes before producing a new vacuum that worked. Even after all of this perseverance, he still could not find an American or European company to license and manufacture his product. In 1993, he created his own manufacturing operation and within 2 years, Dyson vacuums were a worldwide sensation.

GROWTH MINDSET

In her book, *Mindset: The New Psychology of Success*, Carol Dweck explains that her research of over 20 years has "shown that the view you adopt for yourself profoundly affects the way you lead your life. It can determine whether you become the person you want to be and whether you accomplish the things you value."[1] Initially observing how children approached solving hard problems to understand how people cope with failures, she saw children approach these problems with enjoyment, relishing the challenge and seeing failure as an opportunity to learn. Her research explains the difference between a fixed and a growth mindset and is now so well known it is incorporated into many primary school curriculums in Australia and displayed on posters on classroom walls. A fixed mindset believes that human qualities, such as intelligence or talent, are set or static, whereas a growth mindset believes that, with effort, capabilities, talents and intelligence can be developed.

This research and theory is valuable in many settings. In primary schools they are using it to help children re-frame their attitudes and approaches to learning. For example, instead of saying "This maths problem is too hard" they are encouraged reframe it to "I find maths challenging, and with effort and practice I will improve." The power of "yet" is often discussed: "I don't know how to work this out *yet*, but I will get help and find a way."

Dweck talks about the fixed mindset, which can lead to a low effort syndrome: rather than learning, we simply don't try for fear of failure or looking stupid. Making a career change and navigating the job market is a process and a skill you can learn and get better at.

Dweck places a strong emphasis on effort: in both personal and professional life it is important to reward and praise the effort, rather than the intelligence or the outcome on its own. In re-evaluating your career and making a change, this focus on effort over outcome and persisting through setbacks is important because this type of change rarely happens on the first try and learning from setbacks is a part of the journey. As legendary baseball player Babe Ruth said, "Every strike brings me closer to the next home run." You can adopt this same view for the interview and job application process.

The business manager example in Chapter 7 was not very proficient at safety. If asked in interview, this could be seen as a weakness, especially if it were a key requirement of the role that you need to have a strong knowledge of and practical experience in safety. Two views can be adopted here, either "I don't know enough about safety, so I won't be able to make a change" OR "I don't know a lot about safety yet, but I am interested and will put the time and effort in to learn more."

With the goal of securing more satisfying work, we advise in Chapter 5, "Flow," that some challenge is necessary. If something is too easy and provides no challenge it will likely be boring. Therefore, you will need to learn new, or improve on existing, capabilities in order to make a change and hence you need to adopt an attitude and belief that with effort you can develop and grow.

Given advancements in technology, industry disruption and the constant requirement to adapt as work changes, this continual focus on learning and development will be critical. While we all can slip into a fixed mindset at times, the tools and advice Dweck provides in her book help people be successful both personally and professionally. On occasion, I have seen some misuse in the application of a growth mindset in the workplace, such as using it to decide who would be made redundant; however, the selected individuals were never given feedback or an opportunity to improve. This demonstrates that all tools and approaches need to be used in context and with understanding.

Dweck regularly refers to the power and impact that just being aware of the fixed and growth mindset can have. Your mindset guides how you interpret information and events. As humans we are advanced sorting machines, always assessing, sorting and monitoring what is going on. The difference is what we tell ourselves about what is happening and what we do about it.

Take the simple scenario of someone who has an incredibly long daily commute. A growth mindset would view that time as an opportunity – for example, to learn something by listening to podcasts or reading if they were on public transport; or to connect with others by calling a friend or a work colleague, or scheduling work meetings where the required outcome was still achievable over the phone. There's a choice to view any situation as an opportunity or alternatively as an inconvenience or a chore.

I'm not suggesting that you must put up with a long commute, if that is not what you are after. Rather, reflect on the mindset you have when faced with a difficult work or career choice or situation and see where there may be room for growth.

ACTIVITY 11

Mindset Reflection

Reflect back on your career so far. Write down one example of each of the following:

- A challenge you faced

- A failure

- Criticism you received about a weakness, or your own thoughts about a weakness

- Observing someone else's success.

> Can you identify your mindset in each of the examples? Did your mindset help or hinder you? Are there possibly stories or self-talk that you are telling yourself about taking on challenges and stretching yourself? Can you test whether those stories are true, based in fact? Is there a way to reframe these scenarios as an opportunity to learn?

With effort and time, you can achieve and succeed. And don't forget the power of yet.

Your mindset for both identifying and pursuing a career change is critical. It will be normal to have thoughts that are unhelpful or fixed; however, simply being aware of them and using the above questions when this does happen will help move you forward.

GROWTH AND LEARNING

There are not too many missteps or wrong moves from a career perspective if you are focused on what you can learn and gain in experience. Even terrible experiences can help you grow; in fact it's possible that we advance and grow more through challenge and difficult experiences.

A few things to clarify about learning. The consumption of content is not learning. Yes, I'm looking at all of the portals and videos that label themselves as learning. Indeed, you may provide a lot of great content, but content is not learning.

Adapted from Bloom's taxonomy for learning,[2] Figure 3 describes the learning process as a continual and ongoing cycle that starts with the learner participating in a learning activity and importantly bringing with them all that they already know and have experienced.

The human brain continues to have the ability to form new neural pathways at all ages, meaning you can teach an old dog new tricks. The learner starts this learning cycle with the toolkit that exists within:

Figure 3: Learning Process

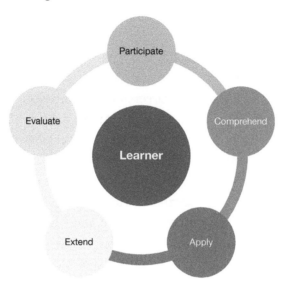

knowledge, skills and experience. So, it is likely there is something they know or can relate to in what they are about to learn. Ideally, any learning you are undertaking assesses your existing skills, knowledge and abilities that are relevant to what you will learn. At the end of the program or course, this should be measured again and hopefully in application after a period of time after the program. In the learning, you will participate (yes, put your phone down even in virtual learning), you'll comprehend the content, apply it through set tasks and then extend and build on it in some way (i.e., given what you have learnt, you can take it in new directions, applications etc.).

Evaluating your learning at the beginning and end of any program you undertake may sound tedious, but it is powerful and practical. Even a simple self-reflection of "I went in thinking I knew a lot, but I had only scratched the surface and there is so much more." And if you didn't learn anything, then well done: you are accomplished and know-ledgeable and perhaps you could give some feedback to the learning provider on how to improve the program.

Apply this understanding of the learning process to formal and informal learning opportunities and you will personally benefit. It will also help you be more selective about the learning you pursue and why, by assessing whether it will help you achieve your goals, whether the pursuit is for the sheer joy of it, or is it because you think you "should" but really have no interest in it.

Your mindset has an impact on every activity you undertake, whether that be an interview, a career or promotion discussion, or when networking. Now armed with the understanding of how the beliefs you hold determine your behaviour, outlook and mental attitude, you can harness a growth mindset to propel you forward. You will be able to learn from any setbacks and to take on new challenges, and instead of being threatened by them see them as an exciting chance to grow.

This focus on the effort that you put in and what you learn from it helps give greater meaning to the various activities that you participate in. The next chapter considers meaning and purpose as powerful motivators and crucial components in the search for more satisfying work.

9 MEANING AND PURPOSE

"Those who have a 'why' to live can bear almost any 'how'."

Viktor E. Frankl, *Man's Search for Meaning*

Most people will spend a large portion of their adult lives working. If you were to sum the total hours spent working, it's likely it would be greater than the amount of time you spend with family, sleep, play, go on holidays or rest. While an activity's importance to you is not necessarily proportionate to the amount of time you dedicate to it, it is however reasonable to hope for and expect that you might derive satisfaction from this investment of your time. A critical way to achieve that is through attributing meaning to that activity.

As humans we are meaning-seeking and meaning-making creatures. In the dictionary, "meaning" as a noun describes what something expresses or represents, or the sense of importance or purpose of the thing being described. For example, "her novels often have hidden meaning," or "when he became a teacher he felt that his life had meaning."

Perhaps you have not stopped to think about the meaning you derive from your work, or whether your work provides a sense of importance or purpose. A lack of meaning in your work could already be painfully obvious, and could be impacting your motivation and level of interest. Getting clear on the meaning that your contribution to work has and having a sense of the purpose or importance of it can positively drive motivation, perseverance and help you be more involved, enthusiastic and committed. Meaning is not static; the meaning you derive from your work is likely to change with the different stages and priorities of your life.

Amy Wrzesniewski, an American organisational psychologist and professor at Yale, interviewed hospital cleaners, who saw their work as more than just cleaning; for them, the cleaning was about helping support patients' healing.[1] In 1961, when US President John F. Kennedy visited NASA and toured the facility, he introduced himself to a person mopping the floor and asked him what he did at NASA. The man responded: "I'm helping to put a man on the moon." These examples demonstrate how the meaning you assign to your work can change your attitude, motivation and satisfaction.

Professor Fiona Wood is one of Australia's most innovative and respected surgeons and researchers. A plastic and reconstructive surgeon and world-leading burns specialist, she has pioneered research and development in burns medicine, including spray-on skin. On her website she describes herself as "dedicated to improving outcomes for burns patients and expanding the knowledge of wound healing." This describes how she views her purpose, and this has motivated and driven her for much of her career.

Professor Wood's purpose is fairly similar to the earlier example of the hospital cleaner's purpose which was "to help patients heal," which demonstrates that deriving meaning from your work is important, regardless of your job or career. Every role in an organisation has an important contribution to make that delivers value to others. It does not matter in what way you contribute, just that you do. You can find meaning from doing things for others and making a positive contribution, or simply from the satisfaction of doing something well in its own right.

As work and life are inextricably linked, it's helpful to look at some of the research and models for creating meaning in life, before focusing specifically on finding meaning in your work.

MEANING IN LIFE

Having a sense of meaning in life contributes to enhanced wellbeing and shields us from threats; that is, *life protection as well as life expansion.*

There are a number of leading researchers, including Michael Steger, Paul Wong and Carol Ryff, who have based their work on bringing together a very large range of findings and research on meaning in life and wellbeing. While they offer different models, there are a number of commonalities between them. They all take a holistic or broad view of wellbeing and support that meaning is vital to long-term psychological wellbeing. Life goals, making sense of the world and how one fits in, and purpose all feature prominently. Balance is also a consistent theme – avoiding extremes or singular approaches – and recognising that negative and positive coexist and that a focus on just one or the other is detrimental. While the term "resilience" may not be specifically mentioned, people's ability to cope with adversity or to endure and overcome are regularly included and are also found to be useful as opportunities for finding meaning in hardship.

Dr Paul Wong is a Canadian psychologist, researcher and professor and has made significant contributions to his field. His findings, based on numerous studies, state that "the worthy life consist[s] of happiness, achievement, relationships, altruism, self-acceptance and fair treatment." His model for what makes for a life worth living addresses three issues for a meaningful life. First, "what people want and how to achieve their life goals"; second, "what people fear and how to overcome their anxieties"; and third, how people "make sense of their environment and respond to situations."[2] Or, in hopefully not too overly simplified terms: what people want, what they avoid and how they make sense of their life.

Wong describes the human "approach-and-avoidance" system. People will approach or pursue positive emotions and goals and avoid threats and negative emotions. Human flourishing is greater when these two systems work together in balance, rather than focusing exclusively on one or the other. For example, imagine the scenario of someone working in an organisation that announces there will be a restructure and job losses. If they choose to only focus on avoiding the perceived threat of redundancy and do nothing about pursuing a new job, whether that be in their existing organisation or outside, they may find they are out of balance. They might spend too much time dealing with negative emotions, and not enough time on their creativity, self-beliefs and creation of future pathways or options. Alternatively, that same person could choose to both approach a goal *and* avoid a threat – that is, work hard to prove themselves valuable to avoid redundancy, while also being pragmatic about preparing for a possible alternative outcome, setting a goal for their next job and expanding their understanding of whether that job exists in their current organisation or elsewhere. This person will likely find that while they experience a difficult time of change, they are taking action to pursue goals and avoid threats.

Wong offers a model outlining four ingredients that define meaning in life: purpose, understanding, responsible action, and enjoyment or evaluation (PURE).

Purpose – Purpose includes goals, values, aspirations and objectives. It is the most important ingredient in the meaning structure because it provides motivation, aids persistence and directs us towards goals. You've incorporated these through your work and life priorities (Activity 6) and identifying your values (Activity 7). According to Wong, "A purpose-driven life is an engaged life committed to pursuing a preferred future."

Understanding – Understanding involves making sense of situations, knowing oneself and effectively communicating and building relationships. By completing the earlier activities you have articulated your sense of self, priority values, strengths and capabilities and what you want to move towards and what you want to avoid (from the Job Satisfaction History [Activity 5]).

Responsible action – Responsible action means acting and reacting appropriately; that is, making choices and behaving in a way that is morally right, regardless of pressures and temptations. In other words, living authentically in accordance with your values and taking action towards your goals. You hopefully already do this in your everyday life, and we will cover making a plan and taking action towards your career goals in Chapter 15, "Bringing It All Together."

Enjoyment or Evaluation – The enjoyment or evaluation component addresses how satisfied someone is, either with life as a whole or in a particular situation: "A meaningful life is a happy and fulfilling life even if the process of searching for meaning may be unpleasant or costly."[3] Wong proposes that if you have implemented purpose, understanding and responsible action, "then the inevitable consequence is to enjoy a sense of purpose, significance and happiness."

The overall goal of this book is to help you achieve greater satisfaction and enjoyment from your career and that it enables what you want from life. As stated above, one of the most important ways to help you do this is to define your purpose.

ACTIVITY 12

Your Purpose, Your "Why"

You have started to articulate your preferred future for a number of priority areas of your life. The career goals you pursue have broader impact and therefore the goals you set need to be an enabler of the life you want. In situations where work negatively impacts other areas of your life, for example, relationships or physical health, it causes dissatisfaction and leads to a lack of motivation, energy and enthusiasm.

Purpose and knowing your "why" has been a popular topic for some time now, with "purpose" defined as "the reason for which something is done or created or for which something exists." The following questions provide a range of ways to help you get clear on your purpose, otherwise known as your "why," as it relates to your work and career. Clearly articulating your purpose can be trickier than it sounds, so I offer a few variations to try.

Review Work and Life Priorities (Activity 6), where you described your ideal job or career. Even if the job title or exact profession is not yet clear, imagine you successfully made a change that saw your career goals become a reality.

- Why would you get out of bed to do that work?

- What impact or contribution do you hope to have?

- Why do you want to make that impact or contribution?

- Do your values align with your career aspirations? (Refer to Your Priority Values, Activity 7). Can you incorporate your values and aspirations into a sentence that explains your "why"?

- Also have a look at your Job Satisfaction History (Activity 5). Is there a theme in the work you enjoyed the most as to why you got out of bed in the morning for that work?

Don't worry about having all the answers and a completely clear picture at this stage; sometimes it can help to focus on just the next step and how that work aligns to your "why." Those of you with longer-term ambitious and lofty aspirations can best set yourself up for success if you are clear on your purpose. Whatever your situation, each job or career change step that aligns to the core of why you do what you do will help you stay more motivated, more able to deal with setbacks and more able to find meaning.

Your purpose can be very simple, such as "to make a difference" or "to empower others." Not only does knowing your purpose or your "why" keep you going, it also importantly helps others decide whether to hire you. Simon Sinek, author of multiple best-selling books, including *Start With Why*, proposes a model called the Golden Circle, which is a communications hierarchy with principles grounded in how humans make decisions.[4] He states that because of how our brain functions, people want to know the "why" first. His model proposes, first "why," then "how," then "what." If you apply this communications hierarchy to a job interview context, the first thing people are keen to understand is your "why." If they know "why you do what you do," then they will know that you are motivated – and they want to hire already motivated people. Then they will want to understand how and what you do, confirming you are capable of doing the job.

Viktor Frankl was an Austrian psychiatrist and Holocaust survivor, best known for his psychological memoir *Man's Search for Meaning*. The book shares what the experience of Auschwitz taught him about purpose and the search for meaning, which sustained those who survived. He said, "The one thing you can't take away from me is the way I choose to respond to what you do to me. The last of one's freedoms is to choose one's attitude in any given circumstance."[5]

In any occupation or profession, you have an important contribution to make. How you create and derive meaning from your life and work is unique to you. It will hopefully align to all of the pieces of you that combine in your whole self – your values, your priorities in life, where you find enjoyment when you play, your strengths, your areas for growth and what you are capable of. Even the challenging experiences you have are opportunities for learning, growth and meaning. Pursuing work that aligns to the whole you and that minimises conflict or negative impacts on important parts of your life is worthwhile and achievable.

Work can also have a positive impact on how you *see* your whole self, as your work identity is an important part of who you are. Chapter 10 looks at how understanding your work identity and the impact it can have will help move you forward and create the meaningful future you hope for.

10 IDENTITY

When you meet someone for the first time at a social event, perhaps a friend's BBQ or a gathering of parents from your children's school, or numerous other situations, one of the most common questions after asking for your name, and which child is yours, will be "What do you do?" It's an innocent enough question, enquiring generally about what you do for work – one intended to break the ice, find commonality or interest and a quick way of making a large number of unconscious assumptions about you.

There are a multitude of ways that you might answer the question of "What do you do?". You might respond by referring to the job or work that you do, perhaps the team that you work in or the person you work for, or you might refer to the organisation that employs you. For some, the response is primarily about their occupation: police officer, accountant, lawyer, doctor, actor, author, artist and so on. And it's likely you'll provide a combination of information, including your role and the organisation. You might also describe other parts of who you are, such as the social roles you play: parent, volunteer, or political, religious or cultural affiliations.

Interestingly, the COVID-19 pandemic has significantly changed some people's sense of work identity. For example, someone working in a supermarket stocking shelves, cleaning or on the registers prior to the pandemic would have simply described the supermarket they worked in and what they did there. During the pandemic, this identity has changed to being on the front line and having an important role to play in everyone's survival and welfare.

Think back to your last experience of being asked the question about what you do. How did you respond? Was it with enthusiasm, easily communicated and followed by a smile? Or did you hesitate, stumble on your words and notice it was not comfortable or easy to say? If your work is changing because you want it to or because the change is unavoidable, did your thoughts and feelings about the situation impact your response?

How you respond to this seemingly simple question points to a very complex internalised concept, which is your sense of identity. According to developmental psychologists, we start trying to establish a sense of identity by experimenting with different roles, activities and behaviours from about the ages of 12 to 18 years. I've noticed this with my 15-year-old daughter, through her initiating exploratory discussions of what jobs she might do when she is older. A year ago, she was keen to be a kindergarten teacher and a ski instructor. An Instagram social influencer was also a passing interest. Now she is thinking about studying psychology, so she can be a social worker with children. She is simply trying these things on, and no doubt they will continue to shift and change. In addition to our attempts to parent her, her social encounters in the world, her school experience and even popular culture will continue to help her form her own sense of identity.

Psychologists define "work identity" as "the collection of meanings attached to the self by the individual and others in the work domain. These meanings can be based on unique individual characteristics, group membership or social roles."[1] As adults we spend a large portion of our time at work and therefore the identity we construct for our work selves can have a significant impact on our sense of self, both positive and negative.

When I was working at Holden, I recall the story of one of the engineers who viewed his pending redundancy as an opportunity to pursue a long-held secret ambition. His dad and grandad had both been engineers and, as a young man, he had followed the same path out of a sense of duty to fulfil family expectations. However, he also knew that his purpose in life was to care for others. The closure of Holden's automotive manufacturing in Australia, the forced change, gave him permission to fulfil his purpose and to change his identity. He could now be a more authentic representation of who he believed himself to be and he retrained as a nurse.

Research supports that possessing a positive work identity is linked with favourable outcomes, such as having enhanced capacity to deal with adversity, increased creativity, better adaptation to new work settings, and higher motivation to take action, resulting in positive outcomes for the business.[2]

In situations where people are made redundant, and especially when entire industries close, what happens to those previously positive work identities when their roles are no longer available?

In the first round of redundancies for Holden's Adelaide manufacturing plant, I accompanied one of the senior leaders as he informed manufacturing workers, one by one, that their role was no longer needed. On this particular day, every conversation was harrowing, and it was difficult to maintain composure and fulfil your corporate responsibility when all you wanted to do was say, "s**t, so sorry mate!" Mature men, many with tough and imposing exteriors, were doubled over in tears by the end of the conversation, lamenting that they were just four weeks away from 40 years of service, or that they had given their life to the company. For some, working for Holden was all they had ever known; it was part of who they were.

As adults, we continue to develop and shift our identity, both work and self, into midlife and beyond. We respond to changing life circumstances and changes in priorities. We relinquish old goals in favour of new ones, we make new plans and pursue new careers or jobs.

Whether your experience and perception of changing jobs or careers is negative or positive, it is important to understand and reflect on the impact this has on your sense of identity. You will be able to move forward more effectively if you can construct or reconstruct your identity as a whole person (incorporating your work identity) in a positive way.

Psychologists have approached research on the self and the concept of identity in many ways; however, key constructs repeatedly occur.[3] During mature adulthood, it is likely you will create a sense of self and identity using a combination of three factors:

1. How you believe others view your key strengths and roles. This includes social roles (e.g., family member, friend, community member, churchgoer) and professional roles (e.g., occupation, organisation, team).
2. Whether or not you are making good progress in achieving your goals and advancing your most important values.
3. The story you craft that explains how you became the person you are, your present experience and your desired future.

From personal experience, I have witnessed the impact a person's strong sense of identity can have. A positive, whole-of-person identity and a positive professional or work identity can propel someone forward, even in the face of adversity and forced change. I've also witnessed the opposite, where people are unable to move forward or are unsuccessful in their job-search attempts because their negative sense of identity holds them back. Usually, I have seen this occur when someone's sense of identity was so heavily tied to their work that they no longer knew who they were without it; or where someone's most recent work experience was negative in some way, to the extent that it significantly impacted their sense of identity. For example, when someone's sense of identity is linked closely with their occupation, and they are forced to change due to injury, lack of available work or other reasons, this can in some cases cause an identity crisis of sorts and potentially lead to mental health issues. If you or someone you know is experiencing this kind of crisis, please seek professional medical support. The cultivation of a strong sense of identity that incorporates your whole self, not just what you do for work, will help to combat this vulnerability, and will help you make a change with confidence and optimism.

To help you propel yourself forward and to avoid potential road-blocks associated with your sense of identity, it's worthwhile spending some time reflecting on your sense of identity, both you as a whole person and your work identity.

ACTIVITY 13

Your Identity

In your journal, answer the following questions as well as you can. Our goal here is to help you construct your identity (both whole-person and work-related) positively, so answer the questions reflecting on your personal life and your work.

Table 10: Identity

Questions	Personal Life	At Work
What role(s) do you play?	For example, son, daughter, mother, father, community member, churchgoer	For example, occupation, organisation, team, role
How do others view your strengths in this role?	For example, courageous, trustworthy, creative, generous, caring	For example, knowledgeable, competent, empowering leader Refer to Activities 9 and 10 (Your Strengths and Capabilities)
What progress have you made in achieving your goals? How has this advanced or aligned to your values?	Refer to Activity 6 (Work and Life Priorities) – you will have made progress in many of these areas over the years – and then see how they correspond to your values from Activity 7	Refer specifically to the work component of Activity 6 and how it aligns to your values from Activity 7 Be proud of the progress you have made
Craft a story of how you became the person you are, your present experience and the future you hope for. If possible, just a few paragraphs, the highlights.	• Past • Present • Future	Refer to the Job Satisfaction History (Activity 5) and craft a story of your career past, present and future aspirations

Adapted from research on constructing or reconstructing your work identity in a positive way, here are a few suggestions to ensure both your work and personal sense of identity help you get to where you want to go and be more positive about it right now.

- Include virtuous strengths to validate the good that you do for others both at work and personally, e.g., trustworthy, courageous, generous.
- Try to cultivate a sense of self-worth, like seeing yourself as competent, capable, accepted and valued by others.
- Recognise improvement, growth or progress in some way that demonstrates positive self-change.
- Try to identify a balanced and/or complementary relationship between your work identity and your personal identity. For example, you might be a leader at work and also in your personal life, such as president of the soccer club.

The above activity helps you define yourself as a unique individual in terms of your strengths and your roles, the goals you most value and pursue and the story you make of your personal and working life so far.

When you begin to interview for jobs or perhaps start your own business, it will be important to convey how you became the person you are, where you are now and the future you desire. When you are responding to the question "tell us about yourself," you can use your responses from Activity 13, primarily from the work column, but you may choose to add things about your personal life too. This ability to tell a compelling story that describes your unique strengths, your values, your aspirations and your work to date will successfully illustrate your strengths, values and capabilities. It will also help others form critical assessments, such as whether or not they like you and can relate to you, whether you will fit in and whether you will be capable of performing the job.

If you are struggling with this concept because you lost your job and you believe that reflects negatively on your identity, let me reassure you, things have changed. A survey of 2000 adults in the UK who experienced redundancy confirmed that 70% feel there is less stigma attached to redundancy as a result of COVID-19's impact on the job market. After the survey, LinkedIn polled another almost 5000 people, 74% of whom agreed there is less stigma. Having over 20 years of experience in human resources and being responsible for both redundancies and hiring, I feel redundancy is a fact of corporate life and more about the reality of business than a reflection on the individual. Granted it still may feel very personal to you, and that is understandable; however, just watch that you don't convey negativity when networking and applying for new roles. It is ok to be disappointed or sad, but if it starts to impact your confidence, your motivation or your emotional wellbeing, please seek help and use the range of mental health support services available.

Now that you are hopefully developing a strong sense of who you are, what you are capable of, and making sure that you have a positive sense of identity, we're moving from an internal focus to an external focus. We will progress from the self to others and how you can ensure you get the best support from your relationships to help you through the ups and downs of your journey to an exciting future.

11 RELATIONSHIPS FOR SUPPORT

Who do you turn to when things are tough or when you have exciting news to share? Is it always the same people, or does it depend on what the news is? The road ahead will be full of wins and losses, ups and downs, acceptance and rejection. Having the right support to help you through this makes a huge difference, especially if you have not been in the job market for a long time, or have spent much of your time doing one thing and you are hoping to make a significant change.

You might be very familiar and comfortable with the work you are currently doing or have done recently. Navigating the job market and making a change is a new skill to learn in itself and it can be uncomfortable: not really knowing what you are doing and what to expect. You are hopefully already well on your way with building a comprehensive understanding of who you are and what you want. Now you need to work with others to help you get there.

One of my coaching clients worked in a small financial services office as the receptionist and client services coordinator. Prior to COVID-19 and the restrictions enforced on workplaces, she had struggled to achieve the flexibility she was after. She had great relationships with some of her colleagues; however, her manager and the human resources coordinator (who had no qualifications or experience in the field) both contributed to what was a pretty unpleasant place to work.

On deciding to start applying for jobs in May 2019, her partner of 7 years responded: "Now is not the time to be looking for a job." She chose to ignore this unsupportive response and invest her trust and confidence in other close relationships. Relying instead on her mum, a close friend and her cousin, who worked in human resources, she got the support and encouragement she needed, including the motivation to try and to persevere through the sometimes laborious job-application process. She rewrote her resumé and was coached through the interview and negotiation process. It was not long before she secured a more flexible role closer to home in what is turning out to be a much more supportive and enjoyable workplace. Now in her 50s, my client's move was not about climbing any ladder, but about achieving the life she wanted to live and how work would enable that, rather than negatively impact it. It certainly wasn't easy having the partner that she lived with doubting her ability and options to change. However, the encouragement of three other close supportive relationships made up for her partner's lack of support. She also chose not to share every detail of her job-seeking activities, to minimise any potential discussions that might bring her down, instead of lifting her up.

You might already understand how important relationships are for support. Research confirms that relationships with others make the most significant difference to wellbeing. Forging a way forward to greater meaning in your work and ultimately greater satisfaction with your career and life will be more achievable with the right support. It's important to consider who best to confide in and brainstorm with. According to Barbara Fredrickson, a leading scholar in positive emotions and the science of happiness, "Flourishing is not a solo endeavour."[1]

There are two types of relationships we are going to explore. This chapter considers your closest and deepest relationships and the next, Chapter 12, addresses your broader networks and connections. If finding meaningful work or changing your career were easy, we would have a simple recipe book to follow (or, as in the corporate world, a long drawn-out playbook). As unique, complex, interconnected humans, there is no one size fits all. So, you must identify who is in your corner and establish how they can help you with the activities so far and with what's next.

If you have unfortunately found yourself unemployed, then we especially want to bolster your support, as poor mental health has been shown to be both a consequence of and a risk factor for unemployment. That is, poorer mental health can occur amongst people not working, which is in part attributable to unemployment.

CLOSE RELATIONSHIPS

Most people are aware of the importance of close relationships and that we routinely turn to others to share both good news and bad in seeking support for everyday stressors and major life events. When we are under stress, friends, family and romantic partners buffer us from difficulties. Simply believing that others are available if something bad happens is enough to have a positive impact on your health. Professor Shelly Gable and others describe this as serving as a safety net to minimise negative events.

Gable has conducted years of research that supports satisfying close relationships are important in both good times and bad.[2] She explains that when good things happen, people will tell at least one other person (family, friends, romantic partners) at least 80% of the time. However, how the other person responds to this can have very different outcomes; it will either build or undermine the relationship.

When you share your good news with someone, even the small wins like applying for a new job, you want the response to be enthusiastic, positive, inquisitive and one that reinforces the potential good. A response like "That is a great first step! How are you feeling about it? Regardless of the outcome, it will be good practice" is encouraging. Alternatively, "There aren't many jobs out there at the moment. Competition is tough. Do you really have the skills for that?" will have a detrimental effect. Even a passive response of "That's nice" can undermine the relationship.

Understanding this will help you identify the close relationships that will best support you through this journey. If someone is likely to respond in a destructive or passive way, they are not who you should be turning to. This can be a challenge when perhaps your well-intentioned parents or partner can be like this; in their mind, they might think they are supportive and interested in what you are doing. Decide how much you share with which people and who will respond in a way that is helpful.

Close relationships that respond in a way that is active and constructive help to increase your belief about your capability to act and have influence over life events.[3] These relationships can also buffer against a decline in this belief, which can certainly happen in the case of job loss or change. In addition, when people respond in an active and constructive way, it builds trust, intimacy and a belief that they will be there for you when things go wrong. The right support from a close relationship can therefore positively impact how you feel, think, motivate yourself and behave.

SHARING YOUR EXPERIENCE

Why share your career change or job-search experience with your close relationships (both the good and the bad)? The sharing of positive events generates positive emotions, such as joy, gratitude, interest, hope, pride and inspiration, which in turn helps build social resources through a shared positive experience. This process is filled with both negative and positive experiences, good and bad, and you need the right support to help you. I want to encourage you to not only share the negative events but remember to acknowledge and share the positive things, even if they are only small.

In her book *Positivity*, Barbara Fredrickson proposes that positive emotions open our hearts and minds, making us more receptive and creative; they build life resources, including physical, intellectual, social and psychological resources. Positive emotions produce optimal functioning in the immediate and long term. Importantly, she proposes the "undo hypothesis" that positive emotions might undo or correct the effects of negative emotions. A downward spiral has been documented in the research literature on depressed moods and the narrowed thinking it produces. Fredrickson's broaden-and-build theory suggests an upward spiral in which positive emotions and the broadened thinking they bring about lead to increases in emotional wellbeing. The effects of positive emotions accumulate and compound over time, contributing to producing health and wellbeing. She believes that building these life resources can alleviate human languishing and seed human flourishing. Therefore, please use the upward spiral and compounding effect of sharing positive emotions and experiences with others to help undo any of the potential negative emotions that might occur for you during this time.

Your close relationships, to use Gable's terms, will provide the safety net in challenging times and the trampoline to help you go even higher in good times. In this journey of making a change to your new job or career, relationships with others are beneficial and will help you not only move forward but lift you up.

ACTIVITY 14

Preparing for Networking With Your Support Person

Choose one or two close satisfying relationships to support you with this change. Share some of the activities you have already completed. You may have already involved them in the values or strengths activities (Activities 7 and 9). Even if they are already fully involved in supporting you, watch for how they respond to both the good events and those that are stressful.

A helpful response is not blind optimism and only positive feedback or praise. In fact, as shared with me during my research, this can be unhelpful and have a negative impact. The old, "You'll get a job!" that has nothing constructive to it can have the opposite effect of encouragement.

In preparation for networking, it will be helpful to prepare a few sentences that explain to others what you are looking for. You will use this information as you network to help you identify and broaden your knowledge of job or career options that will leverage your capabilities, strengths and interests in an ideal context. It is great to prepare and practise this with someone who knows you well and who you feel comfortable with. The sentences you need to prepare are:

1. I am looking for . . . (Refer to the Job Satisfaction History [Activity 5] for the things you want to move towards, such as a manager to learn from, a team environment or an independent role).

2. Where I can use my strengths and capabilities of . . . (Refer to Activities 9 and 10 for your strengths and capabilities and list them as what you will leverage to make a change).

3. I have excelled and enjoyed roles in the past, such as . . ., where I have developed this expertise. (Refer again to the Job Satisfaction History [Activity 5] and list some of your relevant roles or achievements).

Change the wording to ensure it feels natural and easy for you to say, not rehearsed or stilted. Prepare your statements above and then practise them with your support person. Ask them for feedback and suggestions on what comes across well, what are their positive impressions and any suggestions for improvement. Ensure you are able to communicate what you are looking for and the value you will bring in order to get people to help you identify a broader range of job or career options.

While the journey of making a change can have its challenges, on the other side of it you will hopefully find greater satisfaction with your work, expand your future potential and learn a lot about yourself along the way. Your existing close relationships will support you through this change, but it will also be important to invest time and effort into initiating and developing *new* relationships through your networks as part of the journey, as discussed in Chapter 12.

12 NETWORKS

One of the many benefits of working is building relationships and expanding your networks. However, the term "networking" in the context of a job or career change is uncomfortable and awkward for most people. Is the mere thought of networking daunting or overwhelming? Is it something you try to avoid or have had limited success with? If you are an introvert, is networking something you believe you are just not wired for? Or even if you describe yourself as an extrovert who loves to meet new people and make new connections, does asking for help with your career make you feel vulnerable or incapable?

Networking can be defined as the process of interacting with others to exchange information and develop professional contacts. It can occur in many forums, such as at professional conferences, training events (including those online), trade fairs or simply one-on-one by arranging a meeting with a professional contact.

When you are networking, you are not directly asking people for a job. When networking in this context, you are asking for advice and information to help you expand your knowledge and understanding of what jobs and careers might be available and suitable. There are jobs that exist today that didn't exist a few years ago, such as drone designer and social media coordinator, and this constant evolution of the job market will continue. Talking to people to broaden your understanding of what's out there will undoubtedly uncover jobs and opportunities you didn't know existed. For example, I spoke to a young scientist who had spent much of her working career in a laboratory. She had decided that she wanted a change and was hoping to combine her love and knowledge of science with communication and writing about science. I suggested she look at technical writing roles. She had no idea such a job existed, but it is a role that does just what she was after. You'll find people are usually very willing to help you and after you have established a relationship or connection, they are happy to provide advice, for you to stay in contact and to keep you in mind if something suitable does come up.

Another reason that networking might seem awkward for you is that you feel it is one-sided. However, there are mutual benefits when you build a positive connection that helps you make a change and build trust with someone new. The dominance of LinkedIn as the world's largest professional networking platform makes expanding your network and connecting with new people easier than before.

We're going to shift your perception of the networking process from something awkward and uncomfortable to something that is mutually beneficial. There are a number of reasons that networking is so important. First, people are more likely to want to help you if they know you a little. Second, not every job is advertised publicly, or you can be considered for a role before it is advertised. And even if it is advertised, having someone who already works in the organisation recommend or refer you can certainly add weight to your application and put you to the top of the pile for consideration. Prior to COVID-19, most job advertisements in Australia would receive on average over 100 applications. During the pandemic, that number has grown to over 300 (and more in some cases). These figures are likely to settle, but regardless, being one of 100 or more applications is one of the more challenging ways to secure a new job or career, especially if on paper it is quite a big change for you. So, networking and building mutually beneficial relationships with others will increase your chances of making a change.

NETWORKING AND HIGH-QUALITY CONNECTIONS

Instead of jumping straight into the mechanics of how to network and what to say, understanding high-quality connections, the experience of them and how to create them will help with navigating the world of work in a multitude of ways.

A connection exists between two people involving mutual awareness and social interaction. This may be a momentary encounter or over a long period of time and does not necessarily imply endurance, recurrence or closeness. A vast amount of research exists on connections in the context of employees and organisations. Dr Jane Dutton's research and expertise focuses on processes that build capabilities and strengths of employees in organisations and, in particular, she examines high-quality connections that increase employees' and organisations' capabilities. She defines the quality of connection between individuals as life giving or life depleting.[1]

Defining the features and experience of a connection determine whether it is a high-quality or low-quality connection. The experience of a high-quality connection includes feelings of vitality and aliveness, heightened positive arousal and sense of positive energy, feeling of being known or seen and both people being engaged and actively participating. So, why is this important? Evidence exists that having high-quality connections has physical and wellbeing benefits, including instantaneous physiological changes. When you are making a connection with someone, either as part of the job application process or as part of networking and identifying a range of options for your career, you need to understand how to build and strengthen high-quality connections. If the interaction and experience is one of low quality or passive, you are unlikely to get the outcome you are after.

It also simplifies your objective with networking. Your focus becomes creating a high-quality connection, which provides mutual benefits for both parties.

Combining some advice I heard Jane Dutton give in a podcast with her research, some strategies to use include:

- **Engage respectfully.** Everyday behaviours and small gestures communicate that you value the other person.
- **Share** something about yourself, emotional support (possibly not during networking) or resources. Look for uncommon commonalities – a similarity you share that is rare.
- **Ask open-ended questions.** Show genuine curiosity about the person (as long as you don't put them on the spot or cross any lines of being too personal, depending on how well you know them).

Dutton shares that you can't force a positive connection, but you can prepare yourself for the positive potential in the other person and engage in small ways that acknowledge them. It may be as simple as asking for permission to take notes, or being considerate of their valuable time and their generosity with their insights. Her research shows that every interaction we have can leave a trace that sees the other person better off.

ACTIVITY 15

Networking to Expand Your Knowledge of Possible Career or Job Options

An internet search on tips for networking yields about 484 million results. The process of networking is a way for you to expand your knowledge of options for careers/jobs you might pursue. The old adage, "You don't know what you don't know," is true in this case. You don't know what jobs or careers exist that could be a good use of your strengths, capabilities and interests. The continual expansion of new jobs and changes to skills needed in existing jobs will only increase as a result of the acceleration of automation and digitisation due to COVID-19.

Start with your warmest contacts who will be more forgiving if you aren't your articulate best. The approach is (as indicated above) respectful and open. You are reaching out for advice; you're currently building your understanding of what types of jobs or careers exist and hoping they can spare 30 minutes of their time for coffee or a virtual catch up (video is best). When you meet, restate the purpose of the meeting and use open-ended questions, including asking them about their career.

While your conversations are exploratory, don't be too vague or "open to anything." At some point, you will need to let them know what you are looking for. I don't recommend tying yourself too tightly to a particular job title; more being able to explain briefly where you have come from and what strengths, capabilities and interests you are hoping to use and apply in your next move. Refer to Activity 14 in the previous chapter for suggestions of what to prepare. Ask them for their advice and suggestions and whether they can recommend anyone else to contact. Perhaps they could introduce you, even via a group message on LinkedIn.

Your conversation ends with gratitude, and the intention of reciprocity, whether it be something you can help them with now, or some information or connection that would help them with their needs. If there's nothing immediately, invite them to reach out and call on you for assistance when they need help in the future. You will find most people are willing to help.

Start small, aiming for at least one networking meeting a week (more if you are unemployed). I would recommend keeping track of who you have reached out to, met with and whether there is any follow-up. A simple Excel spreadsheet can help. LinkedIn messaging is a good way to approach people you don't know very well and potentially make new contacts when you have a clear picture of what you are after and who may be best placed to help you.

Networking Discussion Example

"Thank you for your time today. I appreciate your willingness to provide insights on jobs and careers in your organisation and the industry more broadly".

"It would be great to understand what's important to you when you hire people and what you look for?"

"I noticed from your profile, you've progressed your career very successfully. Are you comfortable to share what has helped you the most?"

"Thanks for asking about me. I am looking for . . . Where I can use my strengths and capabilities of . . ."

"I have excelled and enjoyed roles in the past such as . . . where I have developed and built this expertise. Are there roles that need these skills and experience?"

"Thank you again for your time today. It has been really valuable. I am really interested in finding out more about X, is there anyone else you would recommend I talk to?"

The isolation people experienced during the pandemic in 2020 demonstrates that we intuitively miss even simple moments of high-quality connection when they don't exist, from a warm smile as you pass a stranger in the park, or the cursory chat as your dogs want to say hello but you need to be 1.5m distance away. What was, prior to isolation, sometimes an inconvenience became something that you didn't know you missed until it was gone. While you can't force a positive experience, at least aim for a high-quality connection for your sake and theirs.

Expanding your understanding of options by talking to many people is what you are after. Research shows that if you can form even a momentary high-quality connection, the experience is beneficial for both people. This new knowledge removes at least a little of the awkwardness you may have felt about networking. And you're now well prepared and know what to say and how to behave during networking interactions to give you the best chance of building a high-quality connection. You're also making a commitment to practising networking, with at least one connection a week. Over time, you will find the experience becomes easier and you'll find what works for you. It may not be a success-only experience, but if you learn from and reflect on what worked well and what didn't you will get better each time. The help people are willing to offer will provide for positive emotions of gratitude and joy. You'll also increase your chances of success by expanding the number of job or career options that could provide for greater satisfaction and enjoyment from your work. You've got your close relationships for support as you navigate this process, and your network is helping expand your understanding of jobs and careers that might be suitable.

In addition to the other people who will contribute to the change you're making, and to your ability to perform optimally and gain greater satisfaction from your work, the place that you work can also have a significant impact.

13 PLACE

"You can design and create, and build the most wonderful place in the world. But it takes people to make the dream a reality."

Walt Disney

Have you worked in the most amazing office or workplace, with state-of-the-art facilities, technology and a fully stocked kitchen? Perhaps you might have visited offices like this and imagined what it would be like to work there. Or perhaps you're a creative and you work in an iconic building synonymous with the arts and creativity, such as the Sydney Opera House, MONA or somewhere that the sheer beauty and architecture of the buildings conjures feelings of excitement and pride.

You might not appreciate the impact the built environment or a particular place has on you, until you no longer work there. You might not be aware of what type of physical work environment works best for you. Or you might assume that your place of work is not really significant, and you can perform at your best anywhere. But context and environment matters. All work happens in a physical environment, a place. Understanding both the physical impact of your place of work and your attitude towards it can improve your wellbeing, opportunities for flow, and increase your productivity and satisfaction.

As humans, we have fundamental needs for comfort; first, for physical comfort and then functional and psychological comfort. From years of experience delivering training programs, I've learnt that it doesn't matter how great the training was if the room was too hot or too cold, the catering inedible, complaints plentiful or the experience suboptimal. Additionally, as humans we attach meaning to a place, based on our own interpretation, and therefore a person's attitude towards the physical environment in which they work has an impact on their thoughts, emotions and intentions.

A colleague of mine, Toni, spent over 4 years working at the Sydney Opera House. When she joined, her manager told her that in most organisations the people are the most valuable asset; but at the Sydney Opera House, it is the building. Everyone who works there is impacted by the history of the place, its "iconic" nature, World Heritage status and the company mission, which is to "Be as bold and innovative as the building itself." In this case, it is the physical environment that sets the standards and expectations for how people work. Every employee holds a very empowering role of being "temporary custodians" of the building and all that it stands for. When Toni's role was made redundant, she describes being devastated as her identity was very tightly entwined with her role at the Opera House. It was very difficult to lose her connection to the place and the people who worked there. As humans are complex and all of the topics we're covering are interconnected, you can see from Toni's example that her sense of identity was connected to both her job and the place that she worked.

SENSE OF PLACE

While Toni's experience at such an iconic workplace may be rare, it does demonstrate the impact a workplace can have from the physical environment and your attitude towards it, both of which have been studied in environmental psychology.

In a study on a sense of place as an attitude, psychologists have defined "sense of place" as a multidimensional construct of place identity, place attachment and place dependence.[1] Place identity involves a person's ideas, beliefs and values about their own identity in relation to a place. This is cognitive – that is, your thoughts about your identity. Place attachment can be described as a positive bond that develops between groups or individuals and their environment, therefore, it is emotional. Place dependence is how well it serves a goal, impacting your intentions to stay at that place or go. In Toni's example, her identity was certainly attached to the place; she was attached to the place and the relationships formed there and she had intentions to stay there until she retired in possibly another 3 to 5 years.

There has been one study connecting the flow construct from positive psychology to place identity.[2] The study found that when flow is experienced within a place through activities that align to a person's goals, values, interests, abilities and strengths, their sense of place identity is also experienced and is significantly stronger. This means that experiencing flow in a place can strengthen your sense of identity in relation to that place.

On an anecdotal level, you might have witnessed this similarly to the way Toni described it, that her identity was entwined with her place of work. When people leave a place of work after a significant investment of time, this can have an impact on their identity and confidence. While this is due to more than just the built environment, it is intertwined with relationships, a sense of belonging, pride and many other factors.

ACTIVITY 16

Your Places of Work and Their Impact

How this may be helpful is in thinking about whether your places of work have had an impact, positive or negative, on your sense of identity. Reflect and write journal answers to the following:

- Think about your last few places of work. Did the environment have an impact on your sense of identity?

- Also consider whether there was any particular attachment to the environment. What was it about the environment that you felt attached to?

YOUR PHYSICAL PLACE OF WORK

Jacqueline Vischer is a professor and leading expert on the physical environment and explains that first people need physical comfort, then functional comfort and psychological comfort. In the Western world, it's estimated we spend up to 90% of our time indoors; the experience of the global pandemic confirmed, if not likely increased, that figure – at least during lockdown periods. Most places of work meet the fundamental needs for physical safety; however, if this is a concern for you or you don't feel safe where you currently work please seek assistance. For those in office-bound work, whether that be at home or elsewhere, ensure the functional set-up is best for your wellbeing. Many workplaces provide ergonomic assessments or have information available. If not, you can do an internet search for advice on setting up your workstation.

For functional comfort, a workspace is designed to support people's tasks. According to Vischer, extensive research has shown that a range of elements can directly affect task performance, including heating and cooling, ventilation, air quality, lighting, windows, noise, workstation size and layout, access to collaborative shared spaces, cleaning and maintenance and safety and security. Her insight to provide optimal physical comfort is ideally to have a workspace that is adaptable, where lighting is adjustable and where environments support constructive and flowing collaboration as well as focused concentration and privacy. Additional research has proven that natural light in the workspace makes people happier and motivated, and that natural elements, such as views of nature and indoor plants, have a positive influence on mental fatigue and a restorative value.[3]

WORKING FROM HOME

Given the significant shifts to the number of people working from home, I recommend taking some of the above insights and applying them to the place in your home where you work (if applicable). Review the following:

- Is it a separate or zoned area within your home?
- Is it comfortable as far as heating and cooling?
- Is your workspace functional?
- Do you have good natural light and lighting?
- Can you see any nature or do you have any indoor plants?

If, like many, you are working on your kitchen table or in your lounge room, try to have some way of separating your work life from your home life. Can you pack it away at the end of the day? Is there some way you can signify when you are working and when it is your personal time? A colleague of mine who found herself working in a space where she also has her own "play and personal time" uses fun party lighting that surrounds her workspace that sits in her lounge area. When she is doing things for herself for fun, she turns the lights on. Others have invested in a stand-up desk that is easy to move around. I purchased one during COVID that fits together like Lego, without any bolts, and is light enough to move from room to room. When I got sick of working in my office, I moved into the lounge room, where the natural light and views are better.

Other former colleagues had challenges with home-schooling young children while working full-time. They created a makeshift workstation in their bedroom, and also found that they had to split their day: work very early in the morning, take time during the day to home-school and then work again later into the evening. Being able to close the door and hope that her sons stayed asleep so she could continue working, while not ideal, certainly helped one former colleague get through that time. Think through what is practical and works best for you.

ACTIVITY 17

Your Ideal Place of Work

Take some time to reflect on your ideal future place of work. Write down where the ideal location would be, what the physical space is like, how it functions, whether there is a variety of places you can work, whether you'd like a mix between working in a building with others and working from home/anywhere.

Your next place of work may not meet all of these criteria, but it is important to think about what works best for you so you can have informed discussions as part of the job-search process. While this is not the first thing you would talk about, they are valuable inputs when you know you are the preferred candidate and are talking through what is on offer.

Reflecting on any previous workplaces and the impact they had on your identity, attachment and commitment has identified what is and isn't important to you in your physical place of work. You now know that physical, functional and psychological comfort is necessary for your ability to perform at your best. And you have tips on how to set up your workspace for greater productivity and wellbeing, provided you have good lighting, natural light, and a view of nature either inside or out. You're arming yourself to be well supported and now well informed to secure your next career or job change. And the good news is, much of this is simple and easy to implement, so that your place of work has a positive impact on your attitude, commitment and satisfaction. One last key ingredient for your recipe for successful and satisfying work is movement. Movement of both your body and your career adds more benefits than just the obvious.

14 MOVEMENT

You are about to start the job-search process in earnest, or perhaps you have jumped ahead and are already networking and sending out your resumé. If you have made a career change before or landed a new job in the last few years, you might remember the highs and the lows. You may already know the joy of making it through to interview stage, of making a rewarding positive connection through networking, or of having someone respond well to career discussions with you and reflect positively on your experience and what you have to offer. Then there is the other side, the feeling of defeat when you aren't successful for a job you didn't really want anyway, which makes you feel even worse. Someone I know was disappointed when she was rejected for a job working in a laundry of a nursing home. She was completely overqualified, and truly had no interest in the role. Its only redeeming quality was that it was close to home and it was a job. The potential employer reviewing her resumé would have assumed this to be an unlikely pairing, a real mismatch. Someone with 15 years of corporate experience wanting to work in a laundry would be quickly overlooked. This feeling of rejection was short-lived, as a few weeks later she secured a role in the building industry that would help her move towards a change in career path and to pursuing a long-held passion in design. While the income was considerably less, the flexibility, location close to home, future career path and the sheer satisfaction of working in a business she was passionate about was well worth it for her.

So how can you sustain yourself through these ups and downs, put your best self forward and build relationships more effectively? Through movement.

Jo was a senior executive with General Motors Holden. She led the downsizing and redundancy activities for her department during the time of closure. To support others and herself during this time, she describes having a good level of self-awareness and knowing the best way to manage her stress levels. Much earlier in her life she had suffered from anxiety and at that time had gotten counselling and learned about cognitive behaviour therapy: the process of challenging your thoughts and providing a rational response. She had developed those skills over time and had also learned that exercise was really important for maintaining good mental health. Anticipating increased stressors during this significant time of change, she went back to daily exercise, making it part of her routine. She keeps that commitment today, after leaving and having had two job changes since. It remains a part of her routine to stay physically and mentally healthy.

As another example, John, a chief financial officer of a pharmaceutical company, realised he was not great at focusing on himself. At a time of significant organisational change, he made sure that he did what he needed to do to perform at his best. For him, it was regular exercise of running, cycling and swimming and generally keeping active. He knew that if he was doing that regularly, he would remain engaged and be better able to support the people changes in the business. At times when he got too busy and wasn't exercising, he could tell the difference it made. When it came time for John to make a job change of his own, this focus on being physically active sustained him through the change process. He quickly secured a new role at a smaller local organisation, closer to home, providing more time for his priorities of exercise and spending time with his family.

Research shows that moving your body has more than just physical benefits. In her recent book, *The Joy of Movement*, Kelly McGonigal brings together a vast array of research to explain that people who are physically active are happier and more satisfied with their lives; have a stronger sense of purpose; experience more love, gratitude and hope; feel more connected to their community; and suffer less depression.[1] This is universal, culturally and socio-economically. And the joys of hope, meaning and belonging are linked to movement (not fitness).

THE BENEFITS OF MOVEMENT

It's likely you are already aware of the physiological benefits of being physically active, including improvements in weight management, cardiovascular health, increased strength, energy and improved sleep. If you have a fairly sedentary job, the need for physical activity is obvious, and yet many still don't make the time or commitment to it. However, the benefits of movement are much more than physical. Your working life and your ability to change jobs or careers rely heavily on your ability to create social connections, your mood and outlook and building trust with others. If you add to the mix the potential additional stressors of change or being forced to change, then the benefits of movement become even more vital. McGonigal's book focuses on *why* people who move are happier and she shares stories and research that demonstrate that regular physical activity:

- Produces brain chemicals that give you energy, alleviate worry and help you bond with others.
- Reduces inflammation in the brain, which over time helps protect against depression and loneliness.
- Remodels the physical structure of the brain to make you more receptive to joy and social connection.
- Activates the brain's reward system, elevating mood and making social connection with others easier.
- Helps you cultivate positive perceptions about yourself, persist through challenges, endure more than you thought and rely on support of others and community.
- Helps you find the energy, purpose and courage to persevere.
- Encourages participation in life through the brain and body.

Moving your body will increase your chances of success with the job-search process by boosting your mood and helping you present your best self in interviews and networking, increasing your creativity and ability to connect with others.

Research shows that it's not a "no pain, no gain" approach; rather, moderate-intensity sessions of 20 minutes or more, three times a week is enough to make a significant difference. You're more likely to commit to regular activity when you choose activities you enjoy. There are also social benefits depending on the type of activity, such as a bicycle ride, a running group or a group fitness program. This activates a neuro-biological reward for sharing and is the foundation for trust. It has also been shown that movement outside in nature brings more benefits, so if you can incorporate some of your activities with others and outside you will increase the benefits.

MOVEMENT AND YOUR WORKING LIFE

While this chapter is primarily about the benefits of moving your body, movement in your working life also has great benefits. Changing jobs brings variety, increases experience and learning, keeps people engaged in an organisation for longer and thus builds a wealth of organisational or company knowledge. There's nothing wrong with staying with an organisation for a long period of time. The key for your own satisfaction, employability and security in your own abilities is to continue to learn and grow and to have some variety along the way (even if it is the same role, but things rarely stay exactly the same, especially with technology advances).

MOMENTUM

If you have ever navigated the job market to secure your next role, you may already know firsthand how challenging it can be dealing with the ups and downs. Keeping up your momentum and effort, while presenting the best version of yourself, is key. Here are some tips for building your resilience and keeping up your momentum:

- Accept that there will be ups and downs. It is rarely a success-only journey. Know that there will be days where you are highly motivated and days where you just don't want to write another application.
- Use your close connections for support, encouragement and accountability. You have hopefully selected one or two close relationships to help you; set up regular catch-ups with them to talk through how you are feeling, the progress you are making and what else you might need to do or change.
- Focus on effort, not outcome. You can't control the outcome, as someone else is the decision-maker. But you can focus on putting in the required effort to increase your chances of success. One application is in most cases not enough.
- Watch for unhelpful thoughts, such as "There are no jobs" or "It is so competitive, I don't have a chance." These negative thoughts can stop you from even trying. Granted the job market is tough, but it is not true that there are zero jobs. There are industries that are hiring and a wealth of free or low-fee training opportunities on offer to expand your options. As we discussed in Chapter 8: Growth, catch those unhelpful stories or thoughts, test whether they are true or based in fact, and find a way to reframe them, perhaps as an opportunity to learn, or an isolated event, or just something that happens sometimes but is not true all of the time.
- Take the time to recharge and replenish your mind, body and spirit. The job-search process is usually a stressful one. If you are taking care of yourself, you are giving yourself every chance of putting the best possible version of yourself forward. Ensure that you're getting enough sleep, nourishing food and activities like yoga and meditation, or whatever you find is helpful for your mind and body.
- Move. Commit to a regular routine of any form of moderate activity that you enjoy for 20 minutes or more, at least three times a week. If things seem overwhelming or you feel a negative mood permeating,

use movement as a way to help you. Take a break and go for a walk, a jog, a bike ride, a swim or even gardening (get active with pulling out those weeds or mowing the lawn). Again, make it something you enjoy, but do something.

Hopefully this all makes sense and is logical; the benefit of moving your body will positively impact your ability to make a change to your career or job. Sometimes it might be the last thing you feel like, but it is an easily achievable way to sustain you and help you to perform at your best. Whether you are making a new habit of being active or you already have a well-established and enjoyable exercise routine, the benefits will soon become evident both for your health and your ability to make the change you desire.

Through the activities you have completed so far, you hopefully now know what you want from life, and how your career or job needs to work with your other priorities. In Chapter 15, we bring all of this together so you can see how all of these pieces create your unique recipe and provide you with multiple options for finding success and purpose-driven work.

15 BRINGING IT ALL TOGETHER

You've started this journey navigating your own course towards satisfying and meaningful work. The recipe and ingredients are unique to you, and in this chapter we discuss how to bring everything together in preparation for your career change. So far, here are the ingredients you've identified for your recipe.

MOTIVATION AND CONFIDENCE (ACTIVITIES 1 AND 2)

Reviewing both your motivation and confidence has made sure you are starting the journey well prepared and won't be tripped up later. For motivation you need "ABC": autonomy, belonging and competence. In this context, these factors relate, respectively, to (1) the belief that you have a choice to make an informed, and not a forced, decision to act; (2) you have relationships to support you; and (3) you have the skills needed to make the change happen. Having come this far, you are well on your way; however, motivation alone is not enough.

We checked your confidence and whether there were worries or fears that would hold you back. It is absolutely normal and ok to have wavering confidence at times. Chapter 1, "Are You Ready?", describes how taking small safe steps will both build your confidence and give you check-in points to catch your fears and hopefully prove that they are just fears, passing thoughts, and not psychic predictions. The process of reflecting on your previous or current role as a relationship has hopefully helped you review your work and working environment from a new perspective, and enabled you to process any emotions that perhaps you are still holding on to.

MINDFULNESS (ACTIVITY 3)

You now have both an on-the-spot strategy for dealing with any nerves or anxiety that might occur during this process and have also hopefully started, or at least tried, a regular mindfulness practice. Mindfulness both improves your performance and reduces potential hindrances that occur as a result of your brain and biology stress response. This pause between your thoughts and your actions means that you can take yourself off auto-pilot and be firmly in the driver's seat, being able to chart your own course. Some thoughts are just thoughts, and not the real you, and your best chance at success is making sure the real you is responding consciously and productively.

PLAY (ACTIVITY 4)

You've compared your early memories of play to how and where you experience that now. It is quite possible that it highlighted a strength that currently shows up in your work and life. For some, this may indicate leadership: they were always the one who liked to initiate and direct the game. For others, they were telling stories and reading as a pre-schooler through pretend and imitation, revealing natural gifts for language and creativity. Still others may have had an interest in how things worked and fit together, which has led them to engineering, trade or technical roles. Finding time for play in your everyday life has benefits, similar to mindfulness, including self-regulation, improving problem-solving, creativity, language and social skills. So hopefully you have found an opportunity to re-introduce opportunities for play more regularly.

JOB SATISFACTION HISTORY (ACTIVITY 5)

The Job Satisfaction History should have captured the conditions, context and activities that contribute to your satisfaction, or lack thereof, with work. The positive factors are ingredients to include in seeking out your next move and the negative are things to move away from or minimise. Often, the negative factors indicate the opposite of what you'd like to achieve. For example, if the reason for low satisfaction was a poor manager who micromanaged or was really difficult to work for, then you are looking for a good – or hopefully great – manager. Think about what that looks like for you. Is a great manager someone you can learn from, who empowers you, provides good direction or allows for great independence and freedom?

WORK AND LIFE PRIORITIES (ACTIVITY 6)

Articulating what you ideally want from various components of your life has given you clarity on the whole picture. Importantly, your job or career is interconnected to so many areas of your life, and what you want from each will be a key consideration in identifying career and job options that provide for greater satisfaction. Each component and what you want from it has a consequence that helps you clarify what you are looking for. For example, when you reviewed your relationships, you may have decided that you want more time with your family; therefore a job close to home or the ability to work from home some of the time will be something you are looking for. Or perhaps, like in an earlier example, you have a passion for home design – working in a related industry would inform some of the job options. Maybe you've decided you want to prioritise and improve your physical health, so changing to a job that is less sedentary could be an option or a job with benefits like gym memberships or the opportunity to exercise at lunch time or before or after work. There are a multitude of possibilities, and while they may seem obvious, the process of writing them down and clarifying what you want helps you be really clear with what you are looking for. It also sets you up for a greater chance of success, as often we simply forget to ask for what we need or would like.

VALUES (ACTIVITY 7)

You've reviewed your priority values and reflected on how they have previously impacted your career or job choices. You'll be looking for work and an organisation that both aligns to your values and where the conditions and requirements of the work won't cause significant conflict with your priority values. For example, if family is a key priority value, however the demands of the role mean that you are away from home regularly and when you are home, you're too tired or stressed to have much quality time with them, then this will lead to an inner conflict and result in dissatisfaction or resentment of your work. Of course, there are times when this happens; there are peaks and troughs in many people's workloads. However, the intention here is to avoid that rinse-and-repeat cycle of finding yourself in the same unsatisfying situation. And while there is no instant fix, being aware of your values before you decide on your next role can help you avoid this. Importantly, being clear on your own values will help you with the application and job-interview process, as when there is a strong connection between your priority values and what is on offer in the job, it not only means a more satisfying option for you, it works in your favour as a real positive from the hiring decision-maker's point of view.

FLOW (ACTIVITY 8)

Understanding your experiences of the state of flow has hopefully helped you identify future activities, conditions and environments where you are likely to experience flow more often, which will then lead to more enjoyment and satisfaction not only in your work, but also greater happiness in your life. Look for opportunities where what you will be doing in your next job is likely to create opportunities for you to experience a state of flow regularly.

STRENGTHS (ACTIVITY 9)

The strengths that make you unique are important to articulate to help identify opportunities to use them in your work in the right context, and also to continue to develop them through your career. Practically, they add the flavour of who you are to your resumé, application letters and in interviews. And again, like finding more opportunities to experience the state of flow, using your strengths more often helps you be happier, have more confidence, energy and vitality, be more resilient, improve work performance and achievement, and brings more enjoyment and satisfaction.

CAPABILITIES (ACTIVITY 10)

Your technical and people skills and knowledge provide the platform to build from and are what you leverage to make a change. You might have identified a weakness or two, along with your strengths. The good news is that if you combine your strengths and capabilities, this can help you address any weaknesses that might derail achieving your goals. We've hopefully convinced you of how important it is to continue to develop your capabilities, to give you more job security, not in the job you are in or change to, but in your own ability to remain employable and in demand. Focus on developing the capabilities that you are already good at and also those that interest you and that you would like improve on.

MINDSET (ACTIVITY 11)

The greatest of strengths and capabilities can only deliver on their potential for satisfying and meaningful work with a mindset that believes and takes action to develop abilities and to persist through challenges or obstacles. Through reflecting on your previous experience of challenges or criticism, you have identified if your mindset has helped or hindered you. Awareness is your greatest power here. Simply being aware of your mindset helps make sure that any setbacks or challenges are seen as opportunities to learn and don't stop you from achieving your goals and fulfilling your true potential.

MEANING AND PURPOSE (ACTIVITY 12)

As humans we are meaning-seeking and meaning-making creatures. Reflecting on the meaning you derive from your work has given you an opportunity to think about what meaning you would like to gain in your next job or career move. Knowing your purpose, or your "why," helps you identify a career or job that will provide for more meaning and help sustain you. It also helps others decide whether to hire you, because they want to firstly know *why* you do what you do, then *how* (your strengths and capabilities) and then *what* (results and value you have delivered before).

YOUR IDENTITY (ACTIVITY 13)

You're now well informed and able to ensure that the identity you have from a work perspective is a positive one that enables you to tell a compelling story that describes your unique strengths, your values, your aspirations and a story of your work to date that illustrates all of this. Critically, you draw confidence from this story and know the value you have to offer. You can't control who will and won't hire you, but you are now comfortable and confident in who you are and have a very thorough understanding of yourself.

RELATIONSHIPS AND NETWORKS (ACTIVITIES 14 AND 15)

You know how to choose the right relationships for support and have established a way that works for you to help you through this time of change. Together with your support person/people, you have prepared how you will talk about what you are looking for as part of the networking process. And you have hopefully begun networking and expanding your understanding of job options that meet what you are looking for. One of the keys to your success is discovering that there are numerous options that will provide you with meaningful and satisfying work.

There are many jobs or careers that can provide you with opportunities to experience the state of flow, to use your strengths and capabilities, to learn and grow and that align to your purpose and values. Remember the examples of Professor Fiona Wood and of a cleaner in a hospital who had similar purposes in helping patients heal? They both use different strengths and capabilities to do just that through different jobs.

PLACE AND MOVEMENT (ACTIVITIES 16 AND 17)

The two final pieces that can have a significant impact are the place you work and the movement of both your body and your career. Your place of work needs to provide physical comfort, functional comfort and psychological comfort (in that order). You know tips for setting up your workspace for optimal performance, like incorporating natural light and a view of nature. Likely, you are already convinced of the benefits of movement, not just physically, but that making a regular habit of movement will help you worry less, form better social connections, improve your mood, cultivate more positive beliefs about yourself and help you find the energy and courage to persevere. And by making a move to something new in your career or job you gain experience and learning, build new relationships and you're engaged in what you do for longer. I hope you are excited by the possibility and opportunity this all presents.

Here's how your recipe looks in a career plan template, culminating in setting career goals or job options and then an action plan to achieve them.

Table 11a: Career Plan

Why you do what you do	How you can make the change	What you want	Set career options and goals
• **Readiness** – Your motivation and confidence to change jobs or career (Activities 1 and 2)	By leveraging your:	• **Work and Life Priorities** – Aspirations for your career and life (Activity 6)	• Create three career goals or job options by reviewing Activity 6. You may want to add or expand on what you completed earlier.
• **Values** – Priorities that drive and inform your decisions (Activity 7)	• **Strengths** – What you are good at and enjoy (Activity 9, and also 4 and 8)	• **Job Satisfaction History** – What you want more and less of in your next role (Activity 5)	• Think of it like gold, silver or bronze medal options. All a great achievement but at varying levels.
• **Meaning and Purpose** – The meaning you derive from your work and your purpose (Activity 12)	• **Capabilities** – Your people skills, technical skills and knowledge (Activity 10)	• **Flow** – Conditons for more opportunities to experience the state of flow (Activity 8)	
• **Work Identity** – The story you tell of your working life so far, conveying the person you are and the future work you hope to achieve (Activity 13)	• **Growth and Mindset** – What you need to learn (Activities 10 and 11)	• **Place** – Your ideal place of work (Activity 17)	• **Gold:** What would ideal look like, if you could have everything you wanted?
	• **Relationships and Networks** – For support and networks for expanding possible options (Activities 14 and 15)		• **Silver:** Take it back just one step, a compromise that would still provide for a great option, and then again for the **Bronze** version.
	• **Mindfulness** and **Movement** of your body and career		

Remember that this is a numbers game, so while you may set a specific overarching career goal, there are multiple ways to achieve that outcome. It won't be through just one type of job or just one industry. I encourage you to consider three options. Think of it like a gold, silver or bronze medal. All are great achievements but at varying levels. For your gold version, what would ideal look like, if you could have everything you want? For silver, take it back just one step, a compromise that would still provide for a great option, and then again for the bronze version.

Use Table 11b as your career plan options and action planning template or adapt as you would like to. The key here is to have a few options that will provide for meaningful and satisfying work and to write and execute actions that will help you achieve your goal. You may find that some of the actions are the same across all your options, or that they differ because your options are very different. For example,

Table 11b: Career Plan: Options and Action Plan Template

Career / Job Options:	Gold	Silver	Bronze
	Doing what type of work? Using what strengths and capabilities? In what industry, location, benefits etc.?	Doing what type of work? Using what strengths and capabilities? In what industry, location, benefits etc.?	Doing what type of work? Using what strengths and capabilities? In what industry, location, benefits etc.
Actions **Start small** • Easily-achieved short-term actions that will help you move towards your goals. • Small actions you can take now, e.g., increase your networks on LinkedIn, improve your resumé and profile, review job ads to understand job requirements and networking meetings to expand options. • Dedicate 30 minutes a day, or every other day, to the above (more if you are not currently working). **Next** • List any new skills or expertise you want to learn. • Options for learning (online, short course, mentoring). • Use a networking tracking sheet and continue networking to broaden your understanding of career or job options. **Longer term** • Are there any actions that you know may take more than 12 months to accomplish? Include target dates. **Potential challenges** • What are the challenges that could get in the way of achieving your goals? • List any perceived barriers and what you need to do to overcome them.			

setting a goal for a type of work, using similar strengths and capabilities but in different industries, may create your three options. Alternatively, your gold option is your dream of perhaps sustaining a living being a full-time writer. Your silver option is that you find a part-time job providing a steady income in a related field where you still get to use your strengths and skills, for example a communications role. And perhaps the bronze option is a full-time role in communications, with enough flexibility that you can still find time to write; or you decide to do that for a few years, saving enough money to then take time off to write full-time later.

Once you have completed your career plan, discuss it with the person or people supporting you. If you have built a strong relationship with a network working in the area or related field you would like to change to, and you feel comfortable with them, perhaps have a discussion with them about your options and the actions you plan on taking. Ask for their advice and anything else they might suggest.

I'm excited for you! And your career or job options should excite you and be something you look forward to achieving. (If not, go back, be bold and revise.) By completing Part One you have a very thorough list of the necessary ingredients for your unique recipe and how you need to use them to achieve your goal of more meaningful and satisfying work. Next, in Part Two, we put it all into action and start navigating the job market with all the skills and information that are needed to open up a future full of possibilities.

Part Two

THE JOB MARKET

16 NAVIGATING THE JOB MARKET

You're ready to tackle the job market. You might have already dabbled tentatively through applying for a few jobs or begun networking, and that is great! Or perhaps it has been such a long time since you applied for a job, you aren't really sure where to start, and you're unaware of all the different ways to find jobs. So, we start this part by making sure you have the full lay of the land and are aware of all your options. With any journey, there are multiple ways to reach your destination and unlike navigating via Google Maps, where you choose one road, with tolls or without, in this case you actually need to be travelling down multiple roads simultaneously to increase your chances of success and hopefully even find delight when you reach your destination.

ADVERTISED JOBS

Advertised jobs are posted on many websites and platforms. The best sites for finding suitable opportunities will depend on the type of role you are after. In Australia, many of the corporate and professional roles will be found on LinkedIn under 'Jobs' and on Seek.com.au. You will also find them on other sites like au.indeed.com, although in my experience the jobs on Indeed tend to be more in the junior to middle

Figure 4: Navigating the Market

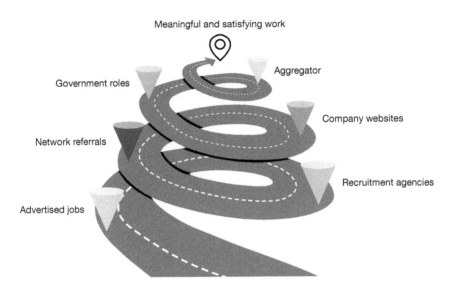

level and the site has many casual, industrial and hospitality jobs. You can also review Glassdoor.com.au; however, you need to register and you must provide a review of your current or previous employer in order to do so. While this is anonymous, you'll need to decide if you are comfortable with this. Glassdoor does also have company reviews about what it is like to work at large a number of organisations. If you read multiple reviews, hopefully you will receive a balanced view; however, I would place more weight in the opinion of someone you know or making a connection in the organisation, than relying on anonymous reviews.

If you are keen on working remotely, try Weworkremotely.com, where companies post remote job opportunities. This site is popular for IT and design roles, which lend themselves to remote work, but there are other opportunities in copywriting, customer support and sales as well.

If you want to work flexibly, then try FlexCareers, flexcareers.com. au, where employers who are committed to flexible working post job opportunities. You may find these jobs are also posted elsewhere, but again its another avenue for you to review. Note, this is not the only site for flexible working roles – many of the jobs posted elsewhere will include whether they offer flexible working.

If you are looking for media, marketing or creative roles, review Mumbrella.com.au, which offers a hub for these industries that you can review in addition to some of the above. For those in the arts, Artshub. com.au has a jobs board for members, and the paid membership offers other benefits.

There are other sites like BlueCollar.com.au, and specialist ones for students and graduates plus many, many more.

The number of job websites and platforms is vast and constantly changing. I recommend you ask people you trust in a similar field where they generally look, as there are also a number of specialist job-posting sites. Once you are familiar with the job-posting sites, you will soon discover which ones have jobs that are most relevant to your search. Most of them also have the ability to set alerts for a particular search, and you will receive an email when new jobs are posted that match the search criteria you have included. This is really helpful, but don't rely on alerts alone. You can find a great opportunity that is really exciting and a strong match for what you are after that perhaps doesn't have a title that you would have looked for, or is in an industry you hadn't thought of, and so forth. So, in addition to the alerts, remember to go back and review the sites you think are most relevant and search broadly on those sites. For example, you might just scan all the marketing roles to see if new job titles are appearing, or search all jobs in a particular location and above a particular income level to see what is out there. Once you have spent a little time exploring, it is likely you will find about three or four sites that you rely on, such as LinkedIn, Seek and one or two specialist job-posting sites.

If all of this seems overwhelming, or you work your way into analysis paralysis where you feel like you are not qualified for many of the jobs that appeal to you, or you have been applying but with no luck, it's best to pause. Step away from it for a day or more, talk through your concerns with your support person/people and watch for the stories you might be telling yourself. It can take many trials and errors to find the right role, but it is only a matter of *when*, not *if*, you will find it. It will happen, it just takes time, good advice, support and perseverance. And advertised jobs are not the only way to identify opportunities; in fact, it is the most competitive way, so be sure to explore the following options as well.

RECRUITMENT AGENCIES

Recruitment agencies can be a key channel to landing a great opportunity. They will post jobs on their own website, and advertise on job boards, such as Seek, LinkedIn and others. Scan their advertisements and create a list of some of the key recruiters who work in the area you are keen to pursue. Even if the advertised jobs are not an exact match for your experience or quite what you are looking for, it is worthwhile building a relationship with recruiters so they can provide advice and also keep you in mind should something come up. Sometimes, when companies don't want the market to know they are looking, or they have been unsuccessful with getting the candidates they want, they will go to a recruiter and request not to advertise. This is where recruiters rely on who they have met with before. It is for this reason that they will often be open to meeting with people for a general conversation even if there is not a specific job opening, so they are aware of you when the right opportunity appears.

Unfortunately, I need to warn you that not all recruiters are created equal. Some will be fantastic, provide you with useful feedback, make you feel listened to and valued and will put you forward for opportunities when they arise. Others, however, will categorise you into a box, and perhaps provide you with poor advice (e.g., "Put a one-page resumé together," or "There are no jobs like that"). They also are often very busy and in high demand from a large number of candidates, so do keep that in mind. However, if you are prepared for the possibility that the experience will be less than favourable sometimes, then hopefully it becomes a little less disappointing and you are a little more delighted when the experience is positive.

NETWORK REFERRALS

Letting your friends and networks know what you are looking for will mean that they can refer you for a job when one becomes available in their organisation or with someone they know. As we covered in Chapter 12, "Networks," a recommendation or reference from someone who already works in the organisation adds weight to your application and puts you at the top of the pile for consideration. Even a general introduction from them to talk to someone else in the organisation who might have future hiring needs can generate opportunities. As you know, everyone gets busy, so don't be disheartened if you see something advertised that your network has not mentioned. It could be that they were not aware of it, or that they just got busy. This is why it is helpful to keep a tracking spreadsheet and to stay in regular contact every few months or so while you are looking. Another good strategy is to expand your network and ask the people you are meeting with to connect you to other people who may be able to help.

GOVERNMENT ROLES

Even if you don't think government roles are for you, I still recommend looking on both your state and federal government job boards. There are some really interesting roles in government departments, agencies and even your local council; it is worth having a look just to understand what is available. I spent a couple of years working in a state government department. The benefits included a strong connection to the organisation's purpose and a feeling of contributing something of importance. The workload was more manageable than my corporate jobs, and there was less expectation that I would work significant overtime. And the people were great to work with. However, I did have to learn the ways of working in government, which understandably had stricter policies and procedures and could sometimes take longer to get things done.

In Australia, federal government jobs are listed on apsjobs.gov.au. The following websites list state and territory government jobs: Australian

Capital Territory, jobs.act.gov.au; New South Wales, iworkfor.nsw.gov. au; Northern Territory, jobs.nt.gov.au; Queensland, smartjobs.qld. gov.au; South Australia, iworkfor.sa.gov.au; Tasmania, jobs.tas.gov.au; Victoria, jobs.careers.vic.gov.au; and Western Australia, search.jobs. wa.gov.au. For local council jobs visit your local council website and they should have careers and jobs information.

COMPANY WEBSITES

If there is an organisation that you would really like to work for, see if their website has a careers page and, if possible, register for alerts and store your resumé in their system. I personally don't know anyone who has secured a role from being stored in an organisation's recruitment database, but this doesn't mean it is not possible. It is also worth reviewing their careers site to find out more about working for them and review a few of the job advertisements to identify some of the common themes of what they look for in future employees. Some will state their values prominently and all their job advertisements will refer to the demonstration of those values. Some will be very committed to flexibility; others may have mandatory conditions of employment, such as police checks and security clearance levels, depending on the roles. All of this is helpful information in your job search.

AGGREGATOR

An aggregator website is a site that collects data from sources across the internet and puts all the information in one place. Jora (au.jora. com) is a job-search aggregator and compiles job postings from other sites, such as Seek, specialist job boards and directly from organisations. You don't apply via this site, but it provides links to the application sites.

Monitor how long you spend looking on all of these sites and whether your time is fruitful, or endless hours of not coming up with much. There is a fine line between being thorough and searching for a needle in a haystack that might never be found on a particular site.

UNDERSTANDING THE RECRUITMENT INDUSTRY

The recruitment industry has no barriers to entry, meaning anyone can hang up a shingle and open for business. The standard business model is that recruiters are paid to successfully place a person in a job, often at a hefty percentage of that person's salary. The reality of their work is that they say "no" to people more than 99% of the time. You may experience some skilled recruiters who will understand your transferable skills and will advocate for you and others who won't.

When I was first in recruitment (almost 20 years ago), recruiters were dictating candidate reports into a dictaphone that went to a typing pool and we provided a detailed report plus candidate resumé to the client. Those days are gone, and now you may find you almost write your own report by answering some additional questions from a recruiter or addressing key criteria in a separate document as part of the application process.

To better navigate dealing with a recruiter or hiring manager, you need to consider the realities of their role and think carefully about how your actions can make their job easier. As a rough guide, if a recruiter (or hiring manager) advertises a job, they will receive 100 applications or more. They review these applications (or an algorithm does) for the candidates who seem to be the closest match to the criteria. When this is done automatically through some recruitment systems, the algorithm is looking for how many times the key criteria were found in each resumé and then recommends the closest matches for a human to review. Generally, they choose between six and 10 candidates to conduct an initial interview. And if it is a recruiter, they will be providing their client with a shortlist of the best candidates, usually between three and five. Recruiters are usually working on multiple roles at one time, so multiply the number of candidates hoping to hear from them, have a discussion with them or be interviewed by them, and you can understand what their job involves.

If you understand you are one of many, you can better prepare yourself when talking to them. The advertisements will usually be clear if they are open to discussions by providing their name and contact details. When you speak to them, be clear about which job you want to talk to them about and explain that you have questions. Be prepared to address any potential perceptions they may have of what is lacking in your skills or experience as well as reinforce the strengths and relevant experience that you offer.

If you are accustomed to going through recruiters for potential jobs, you may have experienced the feeling that you were simply filling a shortlist (the final list of most suitable candidates recommended for review/interview). It is prudent for a recruiter to make sure the client feels like they have a variety of equally good options/candidates to choose from. Like many others, I have had the experience of being upfront about not having all of the required experience for a job, but I've offered different skills or knowledge to be put forward for consideration. In some such cases, I've been given very positive feedback, but I've still been rejected for that same reason in the end. Others have had a very positive experience the whole way, being the final and preferred candidate, only to be trumped by an internal candidate or a situation in which the client loses budget for the role at the final hour. While all of these scenarios can be frustrating and very disappointing, maintaining a professional demeanour will help to build a relationship with the recruiter for the next opportunity.

Recruiters are a very competitive avenue for securing a new job or career change; however, they offer access to opportunities worth exploring. As stated above, try not to solely rely on any one single avenue for identifying and applying for job opportunities.

The options outlined above provide some of the most common ways of finding jobs. Once you have identified a great opportunity that meets your work priorities, will leverage your strengths and capabilities and provides room for growth and learning, you are ready to apply. For a successful application, you need a strong resumé and cover letter, which is what we'll address in the next two chapters.

17   THE RESUMÉ

The purpose of your resumé is to provide information about the unique value that you can offer a potential employer and, if they are advertising for a specific role, to demonstrate how your skills, knowledge and experience match what they are looking for. You want the person, or automated program, reviewing your resumé to find as many reasons as possible to say "yes" to you and as few reasons to say "no." The resumé's key goal is to get you to interview stage. You will usually create it in Microsoft Word and possibly save it as a PDF file if you want to ensure that formatting stays consistent, or so no one can edit it.

There are approximately 132 million results if you search the internet for the "best resumé template." Yet, almost every resumé a client or colleague has shared with me has been less than great. You will find templates everywhere, even on sites like Canva and Envato: both of which I am a huge fan and user of, but not for resumés. Canva is a graphic design platform fantastic for posters, brochures, social media graphics and more and Envato is a marketplace for creative assets from presentations to web templates and much more. Both are proudly Australian-founded businesses. While they can offer a template that looks good, you need to know what to include, where and why.

The type of resumé format I have found most useful and versatile is what is referred to as a functional template, which focuses on your work experience and the skills and knowledge you have developed. Even if you need a different type of resumé or bio, creating a functional resumé is a great place to start and you can then adapt/create alternatives.

There are a few more key things to understand about a resumé. While it needs to be truthful, it is not a full biography and exposé. It is a communication and marketing tool and needs to convey a lot of information about you in a way that is efficient and easy to read. The number of applications for every advertised job varies greatly. And if you are increasing your chances of securing work and, as such, also connecting with networks in organisations before a role is advertised, then you are lessening the number of competitors under consideration. As we covered in the previous chapter, generally speaking, many advertised roles can receive 100 or more applications for one job. The point is not to make this task more daunting, but to better understand the recruitment/ hiring process and also how efficient you need to be with getting your message across if your resumé is one of 100 or more being reviewed.

There are varying opinions about how long a resumé should be. I recommend keeping it to a maximum of four pages; most of my clients' resumés tend to be about three pages long.

Below is my suggested format for a functional resumé and I break it down with explanations of each section and what to include. The overall format is clean, professional, well-spaced, consistent and easy to read. You can elect not to have the side strip of colour, which is included for definition and to stand out.

CONTACT DETAILS

The first section in the template should provide your contact details, with your name, email, mobile and LinkedIn URL for most white-collar professionals. Do not include your date of birth or home address. It is unnecessary for you to include either of these in a resumé and in most applications. Most countries protect people with privacy laws and the data any organisation can collect about them. There are

Name:
Email:
LinkedIn: copy Linkedin URL
Mobile: +61 4

A positioning statement of you and your career. Should answer the three below questions with two to three sentences each, totalling three short paragraphs.

1. Who are you as a professional? (Include descriptive words and key traits, e.g., creative, pragmatic, diligent)
2. What is your current role and/or a key achievement?
3. What is your future focus? (i.e., what are you looking for?) You don't need to list a specific role; it may be a general statement about "Seeking to use my experience to . . ."

CAPABILITIES (list your capabilities from the Capabilities activity and match to job application)

- X
- X
- X
- X
- X

- X
- X
- X
- X
- X

- X
- X
- X
- X
- X

KEY CAREER ACHIEVEMENTS

- Led the . . . (Verbs at the beginning, quantify and qualify where possible)
- Created . . .
- Managed . . .
- Awarded . . .
- Recognised as . . .

> "Amalia is passionate about helping organisations change and grow . . ."
> Name Name
> Title
> Company

QUALIFICATIONS

Qualification (Year)	Institute
Qualification (Year)	Institute
Accreditation	Institute
Internal course	Organisation

RECENT EMPLOYMENT SUMMARY

MM.YY – Current	Organisation	role title (Be generic with your titles)
MM.YY – MM.YY	Organisation	role title
MM.YY – MM.YY	Organisation	role title
MM.YY – MM.YY	Organisation	role title
MM.YY – MM.YY	Organisation	role title
MM.YY – MM.YY	Organisation	role title
MM.YY – MM.YY	Organisation	role title

Only detail last 10–15 years in this summary (unless going back earlier is relevant and worth expanding) also laws about protecting people from potential discrimination. Most medium to large corporate organisations have their own recruitment databases where they may ask you to complete a profile section requiring address and date of birth. However, only provide it if is mandatory (likely only your address). Mandatory sections in an online form are usually denoted by an asterisk or indicated as required. On a second-by-second basis, humans and, even in a shorter time frame, computer programs are making judgement decisions on the information you provide. Detailing where you live may inform a judgement that the job is too far for you to travel to. This, however, should be your decision and not theirs. Ageism also exists and you may be deemed too old or in some cases too young for a particular job. Inclusion of this information is permissible when age impacts the requirements of the role, such as a driver's license, but generally speaking, leave it out.

Sad to say, that even your name and the implied ethnicity of your name will have some people making judgement calls about you. If your background is Asian, Middle Eastern or African, you may have experienced this firsthand in Australia or elsewhere in the Western world. Many people anglicise their names and instantly have better success at making it to interview stage based on the same work history and experience. While this is unfair and totally unjust, and does not happen universally, it is the reality that many experience when attempting to change jobs or careers.

POSITIONING STATEMENT

The next section should include three short paragraphs that provide a positioning statement about who you are, what you deliver and your future focus. You may be familiar with this concept, also known as a personal branding statement or some other term. This is a great way to convey what is unique about who you are professionally, while giving some information about not only *what* you deliver but, importantly, *how*. The first paragraph, usually just two sentences, positions who you are as a professional. Generally, don't limit yourself to your current job title. This needs to expand your job/career options and also position you at the level you aim to achieve or have achieved. For example, if you are a senior leader, then include that as your opening statement in broad professional terms. Add descriptive words that best describe how you do what you do, such as "creative," "pragmatic," "innovative," "strategic," "dedicated" or "diligent." Then expand on that with a broad description of the industry or industries you have worked in and the types of roles. Keep the types of roles as broad as possible and avoid using the term "role," simply state something like "Proven success in applying X knowledge to deliver A, B, C results."

The second paragraph of your positioning statement can lead with your current role and a key achievement, if you are advancing or making a change that is similar to what you have been doing. If you intend to make a change, then perhaps leave it out or explain how your background in X makes you suitable for changing to Y. Add a sentence that colourfully explains more about you as a person, attached to the results you deliver. Use the Capabilities and Values activities (10 and 7) and choose the most relevant to include.

The third paragraph details your future focus – that is, what you are looking for. If you are really clear and it is generally only one type of role, then include it. However, especially for people trying to make a change, keep this statement broad and edit it for every application as necessary. Refer to Activity 6 for what you are wanting for your future job, but remember to couch it from the hirer's perspective and, if applying for a specific job, then it should reflect the role on offer in some way.

From the reviewer's side of applications, it is an immediate "no" if you are hiring for a particular role and the person's resumé reads that they are wanting to advance their career in something different. Keeping this statement broad, it can read something like "Seeking to use my strong people and customer service skills in a supportive team environment where I can contribute and whose organisational values align and are committed to serving others." Change out the skills to the capabilities you identified as strengths and areas of interest in Activities 9 and 10.

CAPABILITIES

The Capabilities activity (Activity 10) is your starting point for what to include here. I use the term "capabilities" here as it is broad and encompassing and you can include people or leadership skills, technical skills and specialist knowledge. Depending on your experience list 9, 12 or 15 capabilities. The roles you are applying for will be asking for these key skills, knowledge and attributes/behaviours. Ideally, you are listing what you are good at and interested in (review the right-hand side of the quadrant in Activity 10). It's likely you will need to expand on this and add any technologies that you are proficient in or have experience in using that may be relevant. Even if not directly applicable, showing you are versatile at a range of technologies or systems says that you can learn and use new systems, which is a valuable skill in itself. This section provides a great opportunity to match the criteria in the job, therefore whether a human or automated system is reviewing your resumé you are obviously matching the criteria in an easily readable way.

KEY CAREER ACHIEVEMENTS

The key career achievements section should demonstrate the value that you bring. It should also address one of the key premises that a recruitment process is usually based on. When hiring, people are looking for confidence and reassurance that someone has done something similar before and will be able to repeat that again successfully in a new environment. No longer are they interested in what you have been responsible for. Just because you have been responsible for something, does not show that you actually did it or how good you were at it. It is like saying, "I am responsible for cooking every night, therefore assume I am a great cook"; however, this is not necessarily the case. Achievements on your first page should be the real highlights of your career and also add any relevant awards, how others recognise you or your volunteer experience. Each should be only one sentence and begin in the past tense with a verb, such as "created," "implemented," "improved," "designed," "changed" or "delivered." As a general rule, most of the content you include in your resumé and especially your achievements should be quantified or qualified in some way. To quantify means to add numbers, percentages, dollar figures, how many people, time frame, and so forth. This helps people understand what you are capable of, adds credibility and differentiates you from others. An improvement in sales of $5 or $5M are both technically improvements. You do not have to give away company secrets or be exact. However, if you led a project that was worth millions of dollars versus one that was worth a few thousand, that positions you differently. Many of the things you achieve in your day-to-day work, previous experience or in volunteering often go by without much thought. Go back to your Job Satisfaction History (Activity 5) and consider the roles that provided the greatest satisfaction. Also think about the most challenging roles you have had but where you still achieved good things in the face of adversity. These are great to include for achievements and demonstrate what you can do under pressure or in challenging circumstances.

If you can't add a number in some way, then focus on making sure it's obvious you are qualified for the job, with the necessary skills, knowledge and credentials or qualifications. Demonstrate how you qualify for the role by using verbs like "created," "implemented" or "delivered," and list relevant courses (even short courses) and your relevant formal education (in the next section of the resumé).

You can choose to insert a text box including a quote from a leader or a client. Please get their permission before you include it, or keep it general if it came through as part of an award or customer feedback. This provides social proof of how you have positively impacted others and the business. This is nice to do, but you will still have a strong resumé without it.

QUALIFICATIONS

Format your qualifications in tabs instead of a table, as some automated recruitment systems have in the past had difficulties reading text in a table format. As it is unlikely you will know what type of technology they use for their recruitment, err on the side of caution, and use tabs to create a clean format instead of inserting a table.

Your most recent formal qualifications should be listed first. It's usually unnecessary to list where you went to high school if you have completed any form or tertiary education, whether that be a trade, a degree or a certificate of any sort. The only exception in my opinion is perhaps at the graduate level. After that I really don't believe it is necessary and again a whole lot of judgement calls can get made based on where you went to school. This can work in your favour or against you, and not always in the way you would assume. Yes, prestigious universities certainly can provide more substance to your application and a point of differentiation against other applicants. However, sometimes it can show you are over-qualified, rather than under-qualified. Perhaps if you went to a prestigious high school and you are seeking a job stacking shelves to get your first job, then an assumption can be made about your ability to work hard. This is all based on bias and impossible to predict, and hopefully will not take place for you. If you have had any experience in applying for jobs, you might have experienced being placed firmly in a single box or category based on something in your resume. This is why giving you the "why" and the "how" gives you the power to decide how you want to represent yourself and show how you can transfer and change to what you want next.

RECENT EMPLOYMENT SUMMARY

As a general rule, the last 10 years of your work history is considered recent or relevant. In the recent employment summary, go back as far as you feel is relevant. Make a judgement call here; however, more than 20 years is probably unnecessary. In some cases, perhaps where someone has taken a career break to care for children, or made a significant change but is seeking to go back to an industry or role they pursued quite some time ago, it may be wise to still include it.

Again, the person reviewing your resumé will make a judgement call about how old you are based on the dates included for your education and your employment history. The old adage of "just because you can, doesn't mean you should" applies here. Meaning just because you have 30 years of experience, doesn't mean you need to include it all in your resumé.

Also, if a role is not relevant or in some cases unhelpful, you can leave it out. For example, a client I was helping apply for a receptionist role at a private Catholic school runs a spray-tanning business in her own time. Given the conservative nature of the organisation, including the name of her business may have worked against her. There are certainly benefits in the experience of being a business owner, such as self-motivation, organisation and strong customer service. We could have elected to leave it out altogether; instead, in this instance, we chose to refer to it in more generic terms as a "beauty business" in her recent employment summary on the first page, and did not detail it in the professional experience section of the resumé (the detail provided in the following pages). In these situations, it is very difficult to know whether this would have made a difference. But it is still wise to think about the type of organisation and business you are applying for and, as much as possible, understand the type of person they are looking for. Whether explicit or not, while organisations are after diversity more and more, they still want someone who will fit in and represent their brand well.

In the footer, add your name, email and mobile. You want it to be easy for people to know how to contact you. The footer is consistent across all pages and while most people will only review your resumé online in a single document, there are times when your resumé is printed; therefore, page numbers and your name and contact details on every page is helpful.

Your contact details, positioning statements, capabilities, career achievements, qualifications and a summary list of recent employment history complete page one of your resumé. As you can see this first page provides a lot of information about you at once. Therefore, at a glance the reviewer knows how to contact you, who you are as a professional and what you are looking for, your capabilities, key achievements, social proof of your value, your qualifications and your work history. Many applications may not get reviewed past the first page; therefore, this format helps to make it as easy as possible for the reader/reviewer to evaluate your suitability and hopefully progress you to the next stage of the process.

The second and subsequent pages of your resumé should detail your professional experience.

PROFESSIONAL EXPERIENCE

The professional experience section begins on the second page. Here, list your most recent role first and then work backwards. Include organisation, role title and time frame, ideally month and year start and finish. Include a sentence that describes the organisation you work or worked for, including its function, size and scope. Even if you work for a well-known brand, this is important, and especially if you, like most people, work for a small to medium size business, then you cannot assume everyone will know what the company does. Size and scope are important. There are differences in working in big and small organisations and everything in between. Small organisations often mean that people have broad roles; they have to do a lot more on their own, perhaps, but can be quick to adapt and change and leverage opportunities. Large employers can have many layers, meaning it can be hard to get things done but someone who works there knows how to navigate a complex system and may often have a very deep and narrow role but looking after larger volumes. All organisations, regardless of size, have their benefits and someone reviewing your resumé wants to find examples of where you have succeeded in the past in a similar environment to the one they have.

As stated above, no longer is it necessary or wise to detail a shopping list of responsibilities. Create a sentence (maximum two) that broadly describes the responsibilities of your role and scope. Scope would include number of people that report to you, client, region, countries

THE RESUMÉ

Following pages on professional experience only need to detail the last 10 years (begins page 2)

PROFESSIONAL EXPERIENCE

Organisation   **Month Year – Current**
Title

One sentence on the organisation – describe its function, size and scope
One to two sentences on your responsibilities in your role

Key achievements:
- Verb – quantify and qualify – include client or project names
- Verb – quantify and qualify – include client or project names
- Verb – quantify and qualify – include client or project names
- Verb – quantify and qualify – include client or project names

Organisation   **Month Year – Month Year**
Title

One sentence on the organisation – describe its function, size and scope
One to two sentences on your responsibilities in your role

Key achievements:
- Verb – quantify and qualify – include client or project names
- Verb – quantify and qualify – include client or project names
- Verb – quantify and qualify – include client or project names
- Verb – quantify and qualify – include client or project names

Organisation   **Month Year – Month Year**
Title

One sentence on the organisation – describe its function, size and scope
One to two sentences on your responsibilities in your role

Key achievements:
- Verb – quantify and qualify – include client or project names
- Verb – quantify and qualify – include client or project names
- Verb – quantify and qualify – include client or project names
- Verb – quantify and qualify – include client or project names

PROFESSIONAL REFEREES   Full details of professional referees available to support capabilities

or industry groups serviced, and so forth. Then move onto listing your key achievements. Include numbers wherever you can, against an improvement, sales or changing a process, which saved time or reduced errors. Without giving away confidential information, include clients or project names if appropriate. If you had budget responsibility, include the total budget figure. All of these details qualify and quantify what you are able to do.

Where you have held multiple roles within one organisation, there is no need to continue to repeat the statement about the company unless there is something specific to a department or branch that would be relevant to your application.

Repeat this format for the organisations and roles for the last 10 or so years, with a maximum of four resumé pages in total.

The last piece of information required is to list your professional referees as available on request. Most organisations will want to speak to one or two referees if you are the successful or preferred candidate, so here you show a willingness to provide them. However, you want to control this part of the process as much as possible. You want to know before your referees are contacted so that you can ensure that they know to expect the call and also to brief them about the role you are being considered for. Secondly, a referee should never be included on your resumé without their knowledge and you want to provide the most relevant and available referees at the time that they are needed. Having worked in the recruitment industry in the 1990s (yes, now I am showing my age!), there was a time where people always provided their referees and some recruiters would use these details to contact and market/sell to referees. This would no longer be allowable, due to privacy laws, as this was not the express purpose for which those details were collected. It's unlikely this would continue to happen and it is more about you having some control over which referees are contacted, when, and keeping your referees personally informed.

Many government or authority bodies will require referees as part of the application. This is the exception to the rule of providing your referee details only on request. If it has been specifically requested as part of the recruitment process, then please do so. Again, ensure your referees are aware that their details are being submitted as part of your application. Getting their blanket permission to provide their details if an application process mandates it is sufficient. There is no need to alert them for every application, as this may be more annoying or unnecessary for them.

Now we've demystified that elusive winning resumé template. You know what to include and how to make a great first impression, as well as how to qualify yourself well for the job and how to stand out from your competitors. Next, we will cover the (sometimes dreaded) cover letter.

18 THE COVER LETTER

"To cover letter or not to cover letter," said Shakespeare, never.

Having reviewed many cover letters in my time, I can share what I believe makes for a great cover letter. Unfortunately, cover letters are not always read, but if you don't put the effort in to write one, that too can count against your application and be interpreted as a lack of effort and real interest. If a resumé passed my first review as potentially suitable for the role I was hiring for, then I would open and review the cover letter. However, if a resumé demonstrated that the candidate was unsuitable, then the cover letter wouldn't be read. As the candidate applying for the role, this may seem unfair. But as the hiring manager or recruiter reviewing hundreds of applications, this is more about efficiency and time management.

The benefit of preparing a cover letter is that it is great practice and preparation in the event you make it past the initial application to the first stage of the recruitment process. While after writing your umpteenth cover letter the process can be tedious, it is still better to err on the side of caution and provide one.

Cover letters should be no more than one page long and follow a formal/business letter template. Unless you work in a creative field where they expect bright and colourful, generally stick to a clean crisp format. A great cover letter clearly outlines how you are suitable for the role and the relevant skills and experience you have that match what they are looking for. Generally, a more formal and conservative approach is recommended: polite and courteous, well-spaced out and easy to read, no spelling mistakes and with the correct details of the job and company. This may seem really obvious; however, I have reviewed many cover letters with the incorrect job title and even company name. Yes, it is likely most letters are a cut-and-paste of a letter you have written before, once you start the application process. However, mistakes like this show a lack of attention to detail and a lack of care and effort. Someone who equally well matches the role requirements and doesn't have mistakes in their letter will be more successful.

On the next page is a cover letter template that I recommend.

Your cover letter should be dated and addressed as if you were posting the letter. Where the role is advertised, you may not have any details of the contact person to address it to. Where possible find out the name of who this should be addressed to. Ideally, this is the person the role reports to or the first person who will be reviewing your application. Where you are unable to find this out, simply include "Dear Hiring Manager."

The first two sentences in the letter are generic, detailing how you became aware of the position and that you believe you are well matched and would like to apply. Adapt this to the context. If you were made aware of the role by someone who already works at the company, that can be great to include.

Next, review the advertisement or the information that details what they are looking for in relation to the role. For most job advertisements, this will be relatively easy to identify. Where they provide a really long list of requirements, group some if possible or select the most critical (often listed first). In this example, a table format has been used. If you are applying to a medium to large company with some type of recruitment technology facilitating the process, use a tabbed format instead. It is not as critical in the cover letter to stay away from using tables and it is easier to keep a nice clean format using one.

In the first column or tab, list the experience, capabilities and qualifications that they are seeking. Then explain how your achievements,

Day Month Year

Full Name on the advertisement or who the role reports to
Title
Organisation
Street Address
Suburb State Postcode

Dear **First Name**,

I read with interest your advertised position of **X** and would like to submit my resumé in application for this position. I believe that I have the desired experience, capabilities and qualifications as outlined below.

Experience/ Qualifications	My Relevant Experience
Experience **(cut down to 2 – 3 words)**	• **One or two sentences that describe your overall experience that matches what they are looking for.** • Over the last **X** years, I have **XX**.
Capabilities or skills **(cut down to 2 – 3 words)**	• **A broad statement that can tie to an achievement or group of achievements demonstrating that your capabilities match what they are looking for.** • Successful results in **X** demonstrates my strong ability to **X**. • **If volunteer experience or passions that you pursue outside of work are relevant, include them also.**
Capabilities or skills **(cut down to 2 – 3 words)**	• **A broad statement that can tie to an achievement or group of achievements demonstrating that your capabilities match what they are looking for.**
Qualifications	• **List that you have achieved the desired qualifications. If it adds to your application, include when and where.** • With a qualification of **A** combined with **No. years of experience** in **X** roles, I have developed strong **X** and **Y** skills.

I believe I would be well suited to the role with **Company Name**. The opportunity to **X (include something critical about the role's responsibility or the company)** excites me greatly and I would very much welcome the possibility for further discussion.

Thank you for your consideration.

Kind Regards,

Your name
Your contact number
Your email

experience, capabilities and qualifications are a match. In the event there is a requirement that you cannot demonstrate, address that by acknowledging, "While I don't specifically have X, my experience in Y and Z provides portable and relevant expertise." There are times when people may not have everything a role is looking for, but offer other skills and experience that would be of great benefit, so can offset or outweigh that requirement. Additionally, if you can demonstrate your ability to learn and adapt in other roles, then you will likely be able to do the same again.

The closing paragraph (two to three sentences) confirms your interest in the role and company and why. I would advise doing a bit of research on the company, google them in the news and see what comes up most recently. Look at their website careers section and review any information about working for the organisation. Things like an alignment of the company values to your own, or a strong interest in the latest products or advancements of the organisation, reflect well in your application.

Some of the things to avoid in a cover letter include using humour or being too arrogant. I have read letters that told me I must interview them, or that of course they would be selected to go to the next stage. This is really off-putting. As a hirer, you want someone who is keen for the role, but not someone who is telling you what to do. It is also not the time to mention salary; this comes later in the process. Some very over-used terms include "self-starter," "dynamic" and "dependable." It's important to give a flavour of your personality, but you can do that through the achievements and experiences that match the job criteria.

In my experience, a cover letter has not changed my assessment of whether a candidate is suitable or not; it usually confirms my assessment and gives me more confidence that the person is worth talking to and inviting for an interview. In some cases, you will be screened briefly over the phone before you are invited to interview. This is another reason why creating a cover letter is good practice, as you will have already thought about how you match what they are looking for. If you receive a call from a hiring manager or a recruiter to ask you a few questions about your application, it is a positive sign that you are under consideration for interview. In some cases, they will want to confirm a few details, question why you are applying, what interested you and what you are looking for. If they call you at a time when you are distracted or busy with other things, it is ok to say that you have a commitment shortly, but would like to schedule a time to speak.

With all of this information, you are now in a better position to be able to go for what you want. A great resumé and cover letter will help you progress successfully to the next stage, which is a job interview. If you make it to interview stage, then both these tools have served their purpose. The work you have done so far will enable you to talk confidently about yourself and what you are looking for. Keep in mind that this process of securing meaningful and satisfying work is a two-way negotiation. The next chapter addresses the interview: how to make a good impression and how to ask for what you want.

19 THE INTERVIEW

Congratulations! You've made it to interview. Now what?

The interview is where things start to become more real. Up to this point, you may have had very little contact with anyone on the other side of the hiring process. And just as much as it is your opportunity to prove you are the best person for the job, it is even more important for you to determine if the job you are interviewing for will meet all of the things you are looking for, in order to secure more meaningful and satisfying work.

Regardless of whether you find the prospect of interviewing daunting or just another meeting, the benefit is you get better with practice. Interviewing well doesn't come naturally to many people. Most find it difficult to promote themselves and talk confidently about their experience and achievements. However, if you understand the process and how best to answer interview questions, you will be better placed to perform at your best. It will become less daunting and may even become something that you start to enjoy.

The reality of the interview process is that, first, people are assessing whether they like you, and then they determine whether you are the best person for the job. I can hear all my HR colleagues disputing this statement: "It's not a popularity contest!" I hear them say. But it is human nature that we look for people "like us" that we like, so we feel safe. This judgement/assessment by the hiring manager is usually taking place unconsciously and once we cover what to expect for the interview process, how to prepare and perform at your best, we'll cover understanding and overcoming bias.

Interview processes will vary. Some will be short and sweet. You meet directly with the decision-maker or hiring manager; it's one meeting, maybe two, followed by reference checks, a phone call or two and then an offer. This is the simplest form (some of you may experience something even less formal than that, lucky you!).

As competition increases and sometimes commensurate with the size of the organisation (size can matter here), the number of steps in the recruitment process can be much longer, including multiple interviews, potentially some form of testing (psychological or proficiency in verbal or numerical reasoning) as well as reference checks and negotiation of the offer. My own personal best in the longest, most protracted, interview process was five interviews: an informal coffee chat with the HR director, then a formal interview on site, a discussion with the CEO, an interview with the people who would potentially report to me, and finally one with the chief operating officer. Admittedly, while the job had been advertised, I had been recommended by a colleague and hence one additional meeting; but still?! On reflection, my fate was sealed when, at the fifth interview, when asked by the chief operating officer what I thought of the organisation (a well-known retail franchise brand), I asked for permission to be completely honest and said "Your hiring process doesn't reflect the values your company espouses. Five interviews causes me to question your decision-making ability. Taking three applicants through at least four interviews, in my opinion, is unnecessary; and, given how the process has been managed, means that likely two out of the three will not be brand advocates." When I didn't get the job, I couldn't be sure if it was due to my candid assessment, or whether they simply went with a less experienced person who was likely asking for a lower salary.

This frank, and perhaps arrogant, response is not one I advise my coaching clients, but what I do encourage is that you view the recruitment process as an early reflection of what the company is like as a workplace. There are no guarantees, of course, but it is a piece of data for your consideration. Are they considerate? Do they treat you with respect and give you the information you need? Or are they disorganised? Are meetings arranged at the last minute? Do things change from moment to moment?

PREPARING FOR INTERVIEW

If you wrote a cover letter or had a job description provided, then you have a good starting point.

Research both the organisation and who you are meeting with. You should have done a *brief* review as part of putting your application together. Going to interview warrants a closer review and research. For most organisations, they will have a website with a Careers or About section. Build your understanding of:

- The company, size, locations and any recent announcements (acquisitions, new products, technology advancements etc.).
- The leadership structure and mix. How diverse is their leadership?
- The company's issues. Scan any annual reports, and do an internet search of news about the company. In particular, this should highlight any prominent issues for the organisation. Issues can present problems to solve, so contemplate whether the issues in the news may have an impact on the job you are applying for.
- The people you are meeting with. There may be something on the company website about them and, if not, they may be on LinkedIn. There's no need to go as far as personal or intrusive cyber-stalking. But do understand who you are meeting with, their background and experience. Recall the information on building high-quality connections and networks in Chapter 12, as this can help you identify something you may have in common, or an uncommon similarity to help build that initial connection. This is one area where assumptions and judgements can be helpful. If their background is heavily technical, you can make some assumptions, such

as they will be data driven, and will like to see rigour and process applied. People with more of a creative background may be more focused on seeing evidence of your creativity.

- The job itself. Go back to the job advertisement or any information you have available.
- Any other relevant topics. Think about questions you have, so you can explore if it will be a good match for what you are looking for. Does is match what you wrote in your Career Plan (Table 11)?

Most interviews are conducted in what is called a behavioural interview format. This is based on the premise that they want evidence that you have behaved and performed in a similar role or environment successfully before and therefore are likely to be able to do that again.

There is a recommended way for responding to behavioural interview questions. Your responses should follow the "BAR" format. You will be asked to provide an example of where you have done something before. In your response, explain:

> B – Background.
> A – Actions you took.
> R – Results.

Prepare responses following this format for each of the key criteria of the job. Ideally, have two examples for each. Especially if you get nervous during interviews, this preparation is crucial. Instead of having to think on the spot and come up with good examples, you already have a library of examples prepared and the only thinking you have to do is to adapt your response to make sure it best answers the question. This strategy has worked really well for all of my clients and, to quote one, gave her "the confidence to put the best version of [herself] forward during interview."

Make sure to quantify wherever you can: numbers, improvements, increases, and so forth. For example, "I increased sales" is a great achievement. However, to make it even better, "I increased sales by

20% year on year, from \$1M to \$1.2M, maintaining profit margin." Adding numbers and data adds evidence that you are the most suitable candidate for the job. Do this for both the actions you took and especially when you explain the results.

QUESTIONS TO WATCH FOR

It is likely the interview may start with a broad open question, such as "Tell us about your background." This is for a few reasons; one possibility is that they have not read your resumé recently and, even when they have, it helps to have you explain your background. Practise giving an overview of your background, highlighting key achievements or projects that you think would be relevant to what they are looking for. Refer to Activity 13 (Your Identity) for what you can include, and ensure you adapt and align it to be relevant for the job.

I've conducted hundreds of interviews. Some people demonstrate that they lack a little self-awareness when their response to this question takes up most of the interview time allotted. Three to five minutes of an overview should be enough.

Other possible general questions include:

Tell us about:

- your strengths (Activities 9 and 10)
- your weaknesses/areas for development (Activity 10)
- your career aspirations (Activity 6)
- what you are looking for in your next role, company or leader (Activity 5)
- your reason for leaving your current or last job
- any gaps in your resumé and why
- whether you have any holidays planned. (This may seem odd, but an experienced recruiter or hiring manager wants to know if they are about to hire someone who then has a long holiday booked at a critical time for the role.)

Watch your body language. Lean in, make eye contact, listen and acknowledge when people are talking. If you are being interviewed by more than one person, share your attention across all interviewers. Be careful that you don't only show attention to the most senior person.

MONEY, MONEY, MONEY

When to bring up money? It is best not to initiate the conversation of money, and definitely not in the first interview. Be prepared that the people interviewing you may bring up the question of salary expectations. Your response can be "I am looking for a salary of $X exclusive of superannuation." Be clear whether the figure you provide includes or excludes superannuation, as this makes a difference. Sometimes, it is easier to say "I am currently on $X salary and would be looking to maintain that at a minimum." If you really want more income than you are presently on, stick with the statement about what you are looking for. I would encourage you not to be too outrageous with your salary expectations, because you can do yourself out of a job; however, it is ok to ask for what you want. Always politely leave it open for further discussion. You want the opportunity to negotiate.

CLOSING THE INTERVIEW

Always have three questions prepared for the end of the interview. It is standard that you will be asked "What questions do you have?" A response of "none" indicates that you have not prepared and are not that interested. Well-considered and thoughtful questions again show your motivation and interest and also say something about you. More importantly, this is now your opportunity to explore if the job, the team, the company and the conditions are a good match for what you are looking for. Your first two questions should be about the job, company or team. Your third question can be about conditions, such as flexibility. But don't lead with this question. Unfair as it may be, it can leave the interviewer thinking you are only interested in the benefits and not really motivated about the job. One question that my clients have found works very well is asking whether there was anything in your responses that needed further clarification to better address the questions or if there is anything else they wish to know about you.

Make sure the interviewers know that you are very interested and excited about the opportunity and thank them for their time. It is also a good idea to ask about next steps, if they have not clarified the process. This helps you manage your expectations on when you might expect to hear from them.

Often in larger organisations there will be at least two interviews. Sometimes the second is with someone more senior or a key stakeholder in the organisation that you may work closely with, should you be successful. Sometimes the second interview is less formal and more of a discussion to get to know you and determine whether they like you and can work with you. Some of my clients have been caught off guard when they have been told that the second meeting would be very informal, only to find that it was quite a formal interview with difficult questions. While it seems unfair to have not properly managed someone's expectations, unfortunately it can happen and so it is always best to prepare. Even reviewing your preparation for the first interview is helpful and again research who you will be meeting with and try to think about what they might be interested in knowing about you.

Remember this is a two-way process. Yes, they need to like you and to get to know you, but so do you. You have a choice and need to be confident that you like them and could work well together. If the manager you would be reporting to does not seem like someone you could work well with, seriously reconsider the job opportunity. In any form of work, your manager has a significant impact on your satisfaction and enjoyment of your workday. A positive experience will keep you there longer, happier and more productive. However, poor managers are one of the key reasons people leave a job. Refer back to Table 11, your Career Plan, and see where there is a good match for what you are looking for and perhaps where there might be gaps.

To recap, here are my top five tips for interviews.

Top 5 Tips for Interviews

Preparation

- Research the company and the people you are interviewing with.
- Check if the company has been in the news.
- Prepare two examples addressing each job criteria.

Respond

- Behavioural interview questions are looking for examples of where you have done something similar before.
- Answer these questions with BAR - Background, Actions you took, Results.

Numbers count

- Qualify and quantify wherever you can.
- Add numbers and data to your responses, even if you can only provide an estimate.
- Repeat the question criteria in your answer, to obviously address the criteria.

Connection

- Research who you are interviewing with.
- How can you build rapport and a connection with them in a short time?
- Is there something uncommon that you have in common?

Leave them with no doubt

- Have questions prepared for the end of the interview.
- Leave them with no doubt that you want the job.
- Be enthusiastic, respectful and grateful for their time and the opportunity.

Amalia
CHILIANIS

https://amaliachilianis.com

UNDERSTANDING BIAS

Every day the human mind makes judgements and decisions. In many cases, this is done accurately and is quite remarkable; however, in the world of work and especially as a job applicant you will be at the mercy of other people's decision-making. Humans make decisions in two ways: intuitively or deliberately through conscious thought.

Referring to the work of Daniel Kahneman and his book, *Thinking, Fast and Slow*, there is a general "law of least effort" that applies to cognitive as well as physical exertion.[1] Therefore, when faced with multiple options to achieve the same goal, people will gravitate to the least demanding course of action.

The way the mind works explains why, in every interview and review of your resumé, you are being judged and categorised by your profession, industry, gender, age, culture and much more. It is automatic and unconscious that someone is making those judgements about you. In many cases, intuitive judgements and decisions are helpful and accurate. But when you are hoping to make a significant change in your career, or striving for something a lot more senior or different to what you have been doing, you can be subject to a whole raft of assumptions and judgements that don't pertain to knowing you, but are based on the person's memory and perception.

Where this can work well is where the decision-maker or hiring manager is well skilled and experienced and also employs conscious and deliberate thought to consider alternatives and challenge assumptions. An unfortunate reality of the hiring process is that decision-makers are often pushed for time, under other types of pressure, or are simply unaware of the unconscious bias they are applying to their judgements and decisions. Additionally, the skill and experience levels differ greatly, inhibiting the accuracy of their intuitive judgements.

If you have ever heard the reason for not being successful in a hiring process was because "of cultural fit," then what you have likely experienced is that "you are not like them" and someone else was *more* like them. Again, it is human nature and evolutionary to feel safe with others who are more like us. This is a constant tension when organisations push for diversity, even hire proactively for diversity, but when it comes to being open to being challenged, considering a different view or needing to expend more effort to engage a diverse team, human nature kicks in and the path of least resistance is often taken or forced.

WHAT CAN YOU DO ABOUT IT?

Acknowledge that you are likely to experience bias and that you yourself also operate this way.

Capture and consciously think about what incorrect judgements or assumptions others might make of your application.

Prepare a response as to how you demonstrate that assumption is incorrect or how you would overcome that potential challenge. For example, if you are attempting to change industries and it is clear that they have a preference for industry experience, acknowledge their requirement, and explain that you have learnt new industries or navigated new environments quickly in the past. State that you have already begun industry research and outline how you would go about learning what you need to know. Additionally, highlight the strengths or similarities that your experience has taught you.

Have strategies that work for you in bouncing back or advancing through setbacks or experiences of unfair judgements.

Cognitive bias is something every person has, that is both useful and harmful, goes silent and yet is obvious, and we both perpetrate and experience it. While you will experience it as part of the interview process, it can be both helpful and a hindrance. However, acknowledging it and understanding it can help you overcome bias if it stands to potentially impact you being able to achieve your goals. And in time, with everything you now have in your kit bag, you will overcome challenges and be successful in your pursuit of making a change to more meaningful and satisfying work.

20 THE OFFER

It will be just a matter of time until you are the preferred candidate and are ecstatic to be successful. It feels good to be wanted, to be rewarded for your efforts in the job-search process and hopefully the job and the offer is everything you are after and more. The interview process would have given you the chance to explore whether the job, the people you would be working with and the company would provide for more meaningful and satisfying work.

Now is a good time to go back and review the Career Plan you put together, Table 11. This time, you will probably look at it from a different perspective. Try using it to evaluate the job on offer. With what you know about the job, the team and the company, reflect on the following:

Values – Does it align to your values? Do the company values and what the company does for its core business align to your own?

Meaning and purpose – Would this work enable you to derive positive meaning? Does it align to your sense of purpose (Activity 12)?

Work identity – Imagine you take on this job successfully. What is the work identity you would create from this (refer to Activity 13 for a reminder)? And would this new work identity complement your whole-of-person sense of identity?

Strengths – Are you able to use and develop your strengths and does the work still provide for some challenge (Activity 9, and also 4 and 8)?

Capabilities – Will you have the opportunity to develop your skills and knowledge and to learn new capabilities (Activity 10)?

Growth – Will this role add something new to your background? Will you continue to learn and grow?

Connections – Is there potential for forming effective working relationships with your manager, colleagues and customers?

Movement – Is your career moving in a direction that will help you achieve any longer-term goals you have?

Work–life priorities – Will the work and conditions enable your goals and aspirations for the other priorities in your life?

Job satisfaction – Will you get more of what you want and less of what you don't? (Look at the insights from your Job Satisfaction History [Activity 5].)

Flow – Will there be opportunities to experience a state of flow (Activity 8)?

Place – How does the place of work match up to what you were ideally looking for (Activity 17)? What works well, what might need changing?

By now, you will have learned that I like a bit of structure. So you can reflect on the above and make a general assessment, or use the checklist below to evaluate if the job on offer is well placed to provide for more meaningful and satisfying work.

Use your best estimate with the information that you have to assess whether the job you are being offered (or likely to be offered) is true for each of the statements below, indicating "yes," "unsure" or "no, it is not true."

This will not only help you evaluate the opportunity, but importantly will point to what you might need to change and negotiate as part of the job offer.

Table 12: Meaningful Work Checklist

		No	Unsure	Yes
Values	Aligns to your values			
Meaning and purpose	Able to derive positive meaning Aligns to your purpose			
Work identity	Creates a positive work identity			
Strengths	Uses and develops strengths			
Capabilities	Uses and develops capabilities			
Growth	Continuing to learn and grow			
Connections	Able to form effective relationships			
Movement	Forward movement of your career			
Work–life priorities	Enables your goals and aspirations for your priorities in life			
Job satisfaction	More of what you want in a job and less of what you don't			
Flow	Opportunities to experience state of flow			
Place	Place of work is desirable			

Scoring

If you answered according to the following, there are some things to watch out for.

Mostly "Yes"

The opportunity looks like a great option. Of course, you can only truly know what a job and an organisation is like once you are onboard and doing the work. However, the initial signs look good. If you tend to be a highly optimistic person, be careful that you have done your due diligence and are not looking at things through only rose-coloured glasses or have made assumptions without validating them. Go back to your work–life priorities and make sure that you are validating that the key things you desire are included in the offer. For example, if flexibility is important to you, yet you have not checked their attitude or policy on flexible working, make sure you clarify that as part of the negotiation process.

Mix of "Yes" and "Unsure"

This is likely a realistic assessment of the opportunity on offer. This is where you should weigh up the impact on your priorities and what you are willing to compromise on for the potential benefits. Look for something more than the benefit of money to offset any potential negative impacts, as we need more than just financial reward to stay motivated, satisfied and successful.

It would be a great idea to test whether the role and company truly excites you and what you would be doing on a daily basis is still interesting for you, with opportunities to grow and develop. If the answer is "yes, it is exciting and you can grow," then it is a good option.

Mostly "Unsure"

It will be critical for you to clarify your biggest priorities as part of the negotiation process. It is ok to request a phone call with your potential new manger or the person offering you the job. Have your most important questions prepared. You can ask via email, but if you have a lot of questions this can come across the wrong way, so I recommend a phone call if possible.

Mix of "Yes," "Unsure" and "No"

There could be potential conflict here. While manageable, balancing an internal conflict regularly can be exhausting. As above, request an opportunity for a brief discussion to understand the work, conditions, environment and team a little further to be clearer on your assessment.

Mostly "No" or Mix of "No" and "Unsure"

Doesn't really need to be said, does it? Not likely to be a great option for you. Even as a stopgap to help bring in some income, there is enough research to support that engaged workers perform better. If it is unsatisfying for you, it will be very difficult for you to do your best and perform well. Not a great experience for you, your co-workers or your manager.

Whether you choose to do the more structured assessment above, or simply talk it through with one of your support people, you should be well placed to identify the key things you would like to negotiate and change about the offer. But how best to do that?

A client of mine found himself negotiating a job offer into a new industry that was offering a significant pay cut. He was aware that the job was paying considerably less than what he was on, as he was changing from an engineering role to a project management role in an industry where he had no experience. Instead of simply accepting what was on offer, he was able to negotiate a smaller pay cut, a commitment to make up that pay cut over time and also negotiate a voluntary redundancy from his employer. (Yes, you can always ask whether there is a possibility to make your role redundant before you leave, just in most cases, do not let them know you have another job secured.)

NEGOTIATING THE OFFER

In my client's case he was clear on what he wanted and had realistic expectations going into a new industry. He was able to explain that while he understood the job paid less than what he was on, he simply asked if there was any opportunity to reduce the gap and increase the pay offer. They met him halfway, as he demonstrated he was still willing to compromise and they were able to stretch a little. In less than 3 years, his performance has proven his worth and has been acknowledged and recognised. He has remained in the industry but has since changed companies and has recently been promoted. He now runs a large department and is in a job he thoroughly enjoys and has well and truly exceeded his previous income level. His advice on negotiating is that you absolutely need to ask for what you want, but importantly it is about when and how to ask.

The early part of the recruitment process is about liking each other, proving your suitability for the role and organisation and being the person they want to hire.

Be honest throughout the recruitment process about what salary you are hoping for, and always indicate that there is some flexibility depending on what else is on offer as part of the package.

Try not to talk about money straight off, unless they ask you. Although, if what is on offer is at an income level that you just can't accept, then best not to waste your time or theirs. A friend of mine was moving from large corporates to a group of medical practices. While the role was comparable, being closer to home, saving on travel time and increasing flexibility was really appealing. However, salary was not discussed until they put the offer in writing after reference checks. It was a $50K pay cut. They were offering less than most graduate jobs. They had wasted her time, her referees' time and their own. This is one of those scenarios where it was necessary to ask politely about the salary range on offer, should they be successful, before going through all of these stages – probably around the time of getting to reference checks. If you experience something similar and are looking at a job that is offering significantly less than what you can afford to reduce down to, be realistic: a gap of more than $20K away from what you want might not be a gap you can bridge. But do think about what else you might value, for example, study leave, investment in further training, reduced hours or more annual leave.

Always start off with a positive acknowledgement. When you know you are the preferred candidate and they want to offer you the role, do not leave them guessing whether you want to take the job. Be grateful and thankful and wait to hear or see the offer in writing. Please remember, nothing is confirmed until you have a contract, and it is not a binding contract until you have signed and returned it.

Unlike the example above, a good hiring manager or recruiter will discuss the offer terms with you before putting it in writing. This is helpful as it provides a better window for negotiating. It is ok to ask for what you want, but be mindful that most companies will have a budget limit or salary ranges that determine what they can offer. This is a time for give and take. What can you be flexible on in return for something? It is not always money that is valuable. Be clear on where your thresholds and limits are and what aspects are non-negotiable. This is a dance, rather than a fight. Maintain your relationships and operate in a respectful and trustworthy way.

There are so many scenarios in negotiating an offer that it is difficult to give very specific advice. View this information as guide rails to work within, stay true to your own values and be realistic while knowing your value and not underselling yourself. Sometimes we don't get to our destination in one step; it can take a few smaller steps in the journey.

Here are some key tips to consider in the negotiation.

- As well as maintaining your professionalism and courtesy, maintain your likeability. You want to keep your future manager, HR contact or recruiter on side.
- Tell a story and explain why you deserve the changes to the offer you are requesting.
- Emphasise how keen you are on the job and working for the organisation.
- Empathise and understand the position of the person on the other end of the negotiation. They will have constraints and requirements of their job that they must meet.
- This topic is about more than money. Flexibility, support for study, additional leave and many other benefits make up a whole package. Be open to finding other ways that you can make the offer more satisfying other than just an increase in pay.
- Negotiate any changes all at once, not one at a time. Asking for one change, and then another once that is resolved reduces your likelihood of success and also likeability. It may also come across as untrustworthy.
- You can ask for time to think about an offer. Just don't drag it on too long. The longer any negotiation process takes, the higher the risk for something to go wrong.
- If you don't get everything you want, but are mostly happy with the offer, remember you can always ask for a commitment to a review in 6 or 12 months' time.

You don't have to take a job just because it is offered. Make sure the people you will be working with, your new manager and importantly the work you will be doing is something you really want and that it adds something to your experience and is heading you in the direction you are interested in.

While a few of my clients have taken initial pay cuts to make a change, more of them have not. Most have maintained or improved their income with their change and continue to progress and advance. These skills of asking for what you want and negotiating a better outcome that works with your life priorities are something you will continue to use throughout your working life. And the better you get at it, the easier it will become and the more rewarding.

21 GOING OUT ON YOUR OWN

Have you harboured an unfulfilled desire to go out on your own? To be your own boss instead of working for someone else? You might think that there are really only two options when it comes to work, either a job working for someone else or a business. But in this complex world, there are many variations on the theme of your own business.

A job is a paid position where you work for someone else, contracted via a range of terms, such as full-time and permanent, part-time, casual, fixed term or short-term contract. Running your own business can take many forms. You can sell a service or a product, be the sole trader or employ others. You can offer your services freelance working for different companies on particular assignments. You can buy an existing business, a franchise or start a new business from scratch.

My parents ran their own small manufacturing business and my first job while I was at university was doing the basic bookkeeping, banking and general errands. It was actually my Mum's business and my Dad joined her; and her Mum before her (aptly named Amalia) also ran her own business, making curtains out of a workroom in Prahran, Melbourne, from the 1960s. It could have been this history, or the fact that I am not very good at being told what to do, that saw me leave a corporate career after 20-plus years to try going out on my own. At the time, I figured it was the best way, if not the only way, for me to do the work I wanted to be doing. My business runs more like a practice, where the services and offerings are largely based on my expertise and I contract in support when needed.

One of my former colleagues, Andrew, was in a unique position where he had the opportunity to take on an existing business that manufactures antennae for recreational vehicles, caravans and campers, after his role at GM Holden became redundant. In talking to Andrew, it was clear that he was very conscious of the responsibility of being a small business owner and employing others. For him, running his business is a commitment to being financially viable for his own family but also importantly for his employees' livelihoods.

"Getting positive feedback and a pat on the back for a job well done is something that you give away, when you change from being an employee to a business owner and operator. It makes it even more critical to have the right support structure in place."

Andrew's breadth and depth of experience has served him well in running his own business. He acknowledges what he is good at and does for himself and who to go to for help and support when he needs it. As well as critical skills, he attributes resilience as imperative for running a small business. His father-in-law gave him some advice that he still lives by. He was a guy who was always tinkering with something, always had experiments on the go. And he would say, "There is always a way to make money. What you have to do is be interested in what people are not willing to do for themselves and find a way to give it to them." He follows this advice to this day; he talks to people, finds out what they want or what problems they want solved and explores if there is a way to add that offering to his business. He's always looking for opportunity, committed to multiple income streams to ensure the sustainability and viability of the business.

IS RUNNING A BUSINESS FOR YOU?

In Australia, small businesses and family enterprises with fewer than 20 employees account for almost 98% of businesses. And as of June

2020, there were still more new businesses entering the market than exiting. According to a report from the Small Business Ombudsman, small business owners report earning a net income well below the average Australian wage with 52% earning less than $25,000 and more than half of businesses having an annual turnover of less than $200,000. While many long for the freedom, flexibility and satisfaction of running their own business, the demands and reality of it are important to consider.

Running a business requires significant self-discipline and motivation. It can be solitary or lonely if you cannot afford to hire people to work with you. You are leaving behind the security of a regular income and potentially, the freedom to go on holidays and truly disconnect from work. It can take years for some businesses to become profitable, so planning and financial modelling will be important to know how long you can afford to invest and pursue your business dream.

In Australia, state governments have great resources, workshops and advice available for small business, so explore what is on offer, for example in Victoria on business.vic.gov.au. You may be eligible for grants or some assistance, particularly as governments around the world are trying to inject funds into the economy to boost employment. Do your research on your market and competitors and put some sort of business plan together before you take the leap and make sure you have the right support in place with a few key close connections to help you along the way. To address the isolation of working in your own business, you can establish a peer relationship, someone who is also a small business owner (not a competitor) but who you trust and who can relate to the challenges, the highs and the lows. It can help to establish regular check-ins to keep each other accountable and motivated. Many of the government resources also offer free mentoring. If you want to minimise your risk, you can always try setting up a side hustle while you continue working to see if it is viable before going after it full-time. While this minimises the risk, it can be difficult giving your side hustle the time, energy and focus it needs to get it off the ground. But you will establish what works best for you.

CREATING MEANINGFUL WORK THROUGH YOUR OWN BUSINESS OR A SIDE HUSTLE

In the rise of the gig economy and the ability to set up your own business or set yourself up as a contractor/consultant in a multitude of ways, you can adapt the checklist from Table 12 to design the work you want to be doing.

Creating Meaningful Work

Think about the business you could create. Write down answers to the following and incorporate them into a business plan.

Table 13: Creating Meaningful Work

Values	List your priority values
Meaning and purpose	What positive meaning will you derive from the business? Write your own purpose and the purpose of your business. Do they align?
Work identity	What positive work identity would you create if you ran this business?
Strengths	What strengths would you use and develop?
Capabilities	What capabilities would you use and develop?
Growth	What would you need to learn?
Connections	Do you have connections to support and help you? Potential partners?
Movement	Does this move you forward in a direction you are happy with?
Work–life priorities	Would the type of business you create enable your goals and aspirations for your priorities in life?
Job satisfaction	In your role as business owner and operator, would you be doing more of what you want in a job and less of what you don't?
Flow	Will you have opportunities to experience a state of flow?
Place	Is the place of work desirable?

This exercise will require some thought and reflection. At times, they may not be easy questions to answer. Just write down whatever comes to mind and then leave it for a while. If you feel comfortable, discuss your answers with the one or two close relationships who are supporting you through this and definitely use the free resources available through your state and local governments.

There are a lot of benefits to running your own business, including choosing the work you do, when and how you do it and who you work with. While it can take a little time for it to be viable, all the work you have done so far will help you achieve your goals. Regardless of the outcome, the priority is to try, to never leave this life thinking about "could of" or "what if?" or "wish I had." You are incredibly capable and people in the world need what you have to offer, in whatever way you choose to offer it, whether that is in your business or in someone else's. The journey of this change to more meaningful and satisfying work is very close to you arriving at your next destination. To sustain you and help make changes again in your future, we'll look at perseverance and grit.

22 IF AT FIRST YOU DON'T SUCCEED . . .

Anyone looking to make a change from what they have been doing previously may find that it takes a few steps to get there. There are not too many wrong decisions you can make, as long as you are moving forward, learning and adding to your capabilities and experience. Often it is the missteps in your career or job changes that help you confirm what is really important.

Narelle was at a general manager level in the automotive industry with customer experience, marketing and warehousing and logistics expertise. She had been made redundant and was approached by Deloitte through LinkedIn to work in their consulting business. The negotiation was quite drawn out, well over 3 months, and she ended up being made redundant and not knowing if she had a job to go to, which she found really nerve-wracking. She describes a lot of sleepless nights, especially as the sole breadwinner raising two boys. The role with Deloitte ultimately fell into place and she fitted in very well with the team and felt she was adding value. However, soon after starting she became concerned that the job wasn't sustainable and it was unclear how she would be successful there long-term. She realised that at Deloitte your business is built around selling your ideas; whereas much of her career had been about percolating ideas with a team to solve a big complex problem, and then developing and delivering those ideas. And it was that satisfaction of building and implementing that she loved.

As she watched the firm put her name and picture on everything, she got a sinking feeling. She didn't want to let anyone down, but it was very clear to her that she couldn't be successful there. She'd taken a pay cut to join Deloitte and that had also started having an impact on her standard and quality of living. She was looking at ways to reduce costs, and exploring how to advance her career to increase her income. She admits she had not really understood how a partner organisation worked. While the job offer came with a promise to fast-track her to partner, it was not until she joined that she could fully understand what was involved both internally and externally. After six weeks, she was again having sleepless nights and just couldn't see how it was going to work. She resigned and although they tried hard to convince her to stay longer and give it more of a go, she just knew it wasn't right.

She left Deloitte at the end of December and in the new year she secured and started a role with a former supplier, a roadside assistance provider. They were looking for someone with sales experience, and although she did not have a lot of sales experience, everything she was able to bring to the role enabled the organisation to expand the role to include sales, marketing, operations and client services.

Narelle's experience is a great example of learning from missteps, of being brave when you know the job's not right for you and of resilience. It shows that sometimes you take on a job that turns out is just not right for you and no matter what you do, there is not a way to make it work. She was brave enough to make this call early, rather than set herself up for a painful experience where she was unlikely to be successful. This may not be everyone's experience, but often in cases where people are making a significant change in their career, it can take a few jobs, a few steps, to land a job that is a great fit and provides for satisfying and rewarding work.

GRIT

Angela Duckworth is best known for her work on grit. In her book, *Grit: The Power of Passion and Perseverance*, she defines grit as the "combination of passion, resilience, determination and focus that allows a person to pursue their goals, even when uncomfortable and seeing little progress."[1] The job-search process is certainly one that requires grit, perseverance and determination to keep going even after failure and rejection. Unfortunately, talent alone does not predict success. Those who are determined to persevere will ultimately succeed. Duckworth refers to consistent effort and states that effort actually counts twice, as effort improves skill and makes you productive. The more you work the job market and pursuing your next job or career, the more you improve your skills in being able to do this again when you need to. And coming back to the numbers game, the more options you pursue, the greater your chances of success.

According to Duckworth, four assets enable grit to develop within:

1. Interest – Like what you do.
2. Practice – Practice daily.
3. Purpose – See a purpose in it for yourself and others.
4. Hope – Have hope for it.

In Narelle's story, she was not afraid to change when things weren't working. Importantly she recognised that the interest and purpose in the work was just not there for her. She did not overreact to this setback; she learnt from it and was optimistic that she could secure a job that was a better fit for her.

When you do land your next job or career move, you will find that the tips for cultivating grit work just as well for starting a new job or new career. The learning curve of something new can be tiring, but focus on the things that you like doing in your new job: practise and put in effort, connect it to your purpose and how it impacts others in a positive way and maintain hope. Richard Lazarus describes "hope" as "fearing the worst and yearning for better".[2] It is ok to be afraid of failure, but maintain your desire for a better day ahead.

By making your way through Parts One and Two of this book, you hopefully now understand a lot more about yourself, and what you need for your next job or career change. You are now well on your way to achieving a brighter, happier future, not only for your work, but also for the other priorities in your life. Gaining greater satisfaction and meaning from your work will have a positive upward spiral effect on other parts of your life. And you have made sure that what you are changing to will enable your desired life. One of the greatest ways for you to be inspired and to learn is to learn from the experiences of others. In Part Three, I share a select few of the many true stories I have captured to help inform my research and the concept for this book.

Part Three

INSPIRATION

23 SANDY

Growing up in a small country town, Sandy went to school at 4 years of age and even before she could read, she was a storyteller. Sandy was raised by a disabled mother who had contracted polio as a child, and grew up with a sister who had health issues due to her mum contracting measles during the pregnancy; this was prior to vaccines. Sandy's mother was a campaigner for care with dignity for the polio and disability community, and an early adopter of feminism in the 1970s. Sandy was raised to be aware of the many issues facing women around the world and understands the pressures on women to keep going, especially in the workforce, regardless of their health or parenting commitments.

Sandy studied drama and then professional writing and editing, both outlets for her storytelling and creativity. Her first marriage at a young age, while short, resulted in a beautiful son and was then followed by a second marriage and another two children. She very much enjoyed and appreciated the large extended European family that came as part of her second marriage package. As a working mother of three, she made career choices that worked best with her number-one priority, her family. The early part of her career was at Telstra, in a range of communications and support roles. Her proudest role was as national manager, coordinating delivery of an Australia-wide training program. While she thoroughly enjoyed the increased responsibility and scope of the program, progressing further into management or learning roles was difficult, due to juggling family commitments and the increased travel requirements. So, she returned to executive assistant roles in a range of industries.

Her passion for performing and dance saw her open a specialist retail business (online and shopfront) for 3 years, winning a business award and creating the "Dancers Helping Dancers" initiative to aid a South African ballet outreach program.

She describes the ending of her marriage as a huge shock. She had supported her husband through his own personal challenges over the years, and although they had issues, the ending of their marriage was truly a surprise. In addition to the divorce, she later uncovered financial abuse. Faced with potential bankruptcy and life as a newly single mother, she chose to use what little money she had from the sale of her business to pay her suppliers and, unfortunately, lost her home in the process.

Due to the realities of her financial and family situation, she decided to return to executive assistant roles, being relatively easy to secure and fairly stable. Or so she thought. She has since experienced two redundancies: one fairly rudimentary, the other poorly handled and a little more traumatic. What's often underestimated about the role of an executive assistant is that in supporting senior leaders, an ability to also understand the politics and power plays in the corporate world is an integral part of the job; as is building a strong relationship with the person you support based on trust, commitment and loyalty. This close relationship or association can mean that if the person you work for loses their influence and power in the organisation, then your job can also be at risk – collateral damage so to speak. The last four executives she supported were all women, who were either forced out of the organisation or pushed to almost breaking point with extreme workload and pressures that they felt they had no choice but to leave.

As a way of dealing with being newly single, she returned to story-telling and in 2013 started what went on to be an award-nominated blog. Initially sharing her experiences of sex, dating and relationships as a woman beyond the age of 40, the blog evolved to include features about women's issues. The blogging community led her to meet many incredible and diverse women and allowed her to be involved with writing projects and to be the volunteer media coordinator for the Access to Fashion show at Melbourne Fashion Week. In 2019, she launched a podcast inviting female guests to share their stories in a conversational and relaxed forum.

She has recently expanded her podcast to extend it to a platform – a website, podcast and magazine. This idea was born out of a frustration that she couldn't buy magazines that resonated for her as a woman beyond 40. She wanted to read well written articles about interesting women outside of the celebrity sphere who were doing incredible things. Sandy's platform enables women to tell their stories, female creatives to showcase their talent and allows women to rise. It breaks down stereotypes and gives back to organisations that are already supporting women and girls. Sandy hopes to start a revolution of thinking for women above 40 who are interested in culture, politics, the environment, kindness and the world beyond celebrity clickbait and body-shaming stories.

While she continues to juggle full-time work to pay the rent and support her three children, now adults (but do we ever stop helping them?), she is working towards growing her platform and subscribers in the hope that, over time, she will be able to replace her income, and her magazine, podcast and website, WB40 (Women Beyond 40), will become her full-time job. She doesn't regret the decisions she made to support her suppliers who were also small businesses and sacrifice her own financial situation to do what she believed was the right thing, or the career choices she has made to prioritise other areas of her life. She remains, however, committed to pursuing her passions and purpose in whatever way she can.

"The one thing I have learnt about myself and other women is that we are resilient. The love and constant support of my female community allowed me to stand up time and time again and persevere. I have always found work which has allowed me to support my children and give back to those around me. My career roles didn't always align with my creative endeavours, and writing was pursued after working hours, as is the case with many creatives in order to sustain a living."

Sandy is a true inspiration. The first issue of her magazine was published in December 2019 and has received great support and is growing in subscribers. Her podcast also has a growing number of listeners, and she continues to attract high-profile guests, including internationally renowned and best-selling author and disability advocate Tara Moss. Values have driven Sandy's career and life choices and continue to be a strong moral compass for her. Her purpose is to help women rise and she does this through WB40 and also in her own way in her day-to-day job, supporting female executives to do their best work. She demonstrates a growth mindset through being a self-taught podcaster and magazine editor and publisher. Her strong ability to build relationships has proved immensely important in securing contributors to her magazine and website and she has a great circle of friends who have supported and encouraged her through her journey. I sense the best is yet to come for Sandy, as she continues to move forward with her career and business. What was once just a dream, has turned into a reality that she can be truly proud of.

24 JEFF

Jeff believes his biggest asset has always been effort. When he was 11, he started delivering the local paper for $12 a week. It took him five hours every Wednesday evening and he loved it because he was alone. Aided by his sister, he then worked at KFC and then Woolworths. He started an arts degree and quit after 6 months because, similar to his high school experience, he felt he didn't fit in. His sister was working at one of the big banks and, true to form, she got him a job there too. Starting as a bank teller, which he says he was pretty terrible at, they threw him into "relief staff," driving to one of 50 branches across Sydney depending on which was short-staffed. He enjoyed being appreciated wherever he went, and it built his self-belief. After 3 years, he was promoted to the enquiry counter at a busy branch; then another promotion quickly followed to an assistant branch manager.

In 2000, there was a restructure (later to become the new normal at the bank). His boss sat him down and said, "Jeff, I believe in you. You are going into business banking." And so it was. No questions, just a statement and Jeff obeyed. That year was very challenging. His new manager was awful and hard work wasn't enough. Studying nights at TAFE and working 60 hours a week or more, he was put onto a performance-management plan and told he'd be sacked within the month. However, a lifeline emerged: the piloting of a centralised support team in the city. Looking back, Jeff believes it was a combination of great leaders and a commitment to capability development that made the difference. He blossomed, and was promoted to senior analyst. After performing well there for a couple of years, two promotions followed in quick succession to then lead a team of 16 in the business banking centre. He was just 26 years old.

A consistent theme of being directly appointed to new jobs and promotions continued and he was promoted to manage his own lending portfolio in Bondi Junction. For 4 years, he built relationships with small business owners. He chose his mindset from the start: wanting to learn from them and be there when they needed him. He was invited into their homes, their lives, their hopes and their fears. One thing that was instrumental through these years was the mentorship he received from the in-house credit manager. They car-pooled every day for 2 years, and Jeff picked his brain on everything. Jeff was very successful, but the success became addictive and he couldn't draw a line between work and home life. The time and energy he was dedicating to his work was negatively impacting his marriage.

In 2008, a seismic event changed everything for him. His brother-in-law was charged and sentenced to prison. Jeff's parents and sister continued to choose to support the brother-in-law; however, Jeff found himself unable to support him for the crimes he'd committed and he and his wife were ostracised from the family. He needed to rescue his mental health and marriage, and realised that he could no longer do his demanding job. Despite only needing a few more subjects, he stopped his finance degree and applied for an internal training facilitator role, travelling around Australia.

In 2013, another restructure was on the horizon, and he chose to move cities and go into a general learning role in head office. He relished his new role and challenge, embraced new thinking, had several amazing mentors, and championed social learning and digital collaboration. He experimented like mad and worked out loud through his blog. As part of his change in role, he organised to work a compressed week enabling a four-hour volunteer commitment to the *Big Issue* office every Friday morning. He describes it as the best thing he has ever done, partially because he did make a contribution to many people's experience during that time; but also, selfishly, because it gave him the perspective he needed to learn how to get out of his own head and deal with his own depression. He built relationships with people that sold the magazines who were a mix of homeless, mentally ill, drug-dependent, disabled and living in extreme poverty. "The fact that they were still alive was because of their resilience, and there I was in a situation where I could help enable their positivity about contributing to a society that had held them down. Going back to work each Monday, all I saw was the enormous privilege that most people I worked with had enjoyed to get that position of financial security and professional status. I tried to share that perspective back into my workplace in any way I could, and I tried to get people to view their workplace as a community in the same way as the vendors viewed the *Big Issue*."

During this time, he and his wife were undergoing IVF and after many unsuccessful attempts, they fell pregnant. After so many challenges and heartaches, he knew it was time to put family first. With some advice from an experienced colleague and support from his new boss, he planned his move back to Sydney. When their son was born, he took a year off to undertake a full-time master's degree and be a stay-at-home dad. What was still up in the air was whether there would be a job for him to go back to at the bank after his time off.

When he reflects on his banking career, he feels that in the first half, he was very authentic: a hard worker, unassuming to the point of almost lacking in ambition, loyal and obedient. In return, his bosses invariably supported him and pushed him to step up. It got much more complicated at head office. He was always trying to live up to an image of what he wanted to become. He bravely shares that he was probably running away from the effects of family trauma and using his career to put the distance between him and it. He became much more driven for the next 10 years. Over time and with a range of support and his volunteering at the *Big Issue*, he eventually made peace with his mental health issues.

He successfully completed his master's degree in learning science and technology, receiving a high distinction for his dissertation, hoping it would provide some long-term career stability in his new vocation in learning, which he loved. It is the first master's ever in his family and he's really proud and grateful for those who supported him.

While completing his master's, yet another restructure took place and his role became redundant. He felt free, knowing he could take a payout at the end of his leave. Being in the same company for so long meant he was quite unprepared for presenting himself in the hiring market. After a number of applications and interviews, he took a contract working for a former boss with an insurance organisation. While only short-term, it ended up being an important bridge to what he now sees as the second part of his career.

He's now in a full-time government role, leveraging his previous experience and doing what he loves in a learning role. It is a consolidation of where his career is at; there potentially isn't as much scope for professional experimentation as in the private sector and he can't be active on social media. However, in return he feels he has job security in uncertain times, decent flexibility and for the first time ever feels universally respected professionally at work. The main thing is, it suits his life priorities with a newborn second son. A job where he can truly switch off on the weekends and an ability to not try to draw more meaning and enjoyment from it than what's healthy. He's not as driven anymore and that is actually helping him be a better father, husband, friend and colleague. He still has dreams one day to do a doctorate, but it might just be when he's old, wrinkly and his kids are adults.

Jeff's story demonstrates how your priorities in life change over time. It doesn't make him any less of a great performer at work, now that he values family time and being able to switch off on the weekends. He recognises that there was a time where work was all consuming and it had negative consequences for his marriage and mental health. But he made decisions and took actions to change that, and he is thoroughly enjoying his family life and the new chapter in his career. He shows you that you absolutely can change and choose your mindset, and the attitude and approach he took to his work and his master's proves that. You can also see in Jeff's family situation that his values drove his decision to not be able to support his brother-in-law, which caused considerable distress for him and his wife. After 20 years in banking, it was daunting for him to make a change, but he has benefited in many ways: a better lifestyle, more family time, professional respect and a feeling of belonging at his work, and security. He also shows how powerful it can be to choose what meaning you derive from your work. In his case, there was a time where he chose to make it mean more than what was healthy for him and perhaps it became part of his identity that he needed to change for the sake of his family.

25 MICHELLE

Growing up in Adelaide, Michelle started dancing at 3 years of age, influenced by her Mum's passion for dance and her aunty, a professional dancer. Her Mum, a teacher who later became a school principal, struggled financially as a single parent, and when Michelle was around 14, her Mum questioned her seriousness and commitment to dance. At the time Michelle was unsure, and as it was hard to see her Mum struggle, so she decided that she would quit dance to save money. When they informed the dean of the dance school that Michelle would no longer attend, the response was an immediate "I won't hear of it!" and the fees were halved. This would turn out to be a pivotal moment in her life. Michelle has a clear memory of thinking to herself at the time, "I can do this and I want to do this!" After making this conscious decision, she really focused and worked hard at making dance her profession.

She studied at the same ballet school for 15 years and then auditioned for the Victorian College of the Arts (VCA) in Melbourne. Successful in her application she moved to Melbourne on her own at 16 years of age, living in a hostel, as the youngest of 88 female residents. Transitioning from a close-knit family to communal and independent living was challenging, especially in an unfamiliar city. The VCA had an arrangement with a youth hostel for their interstate students, but it was full and she recalls receiving little support from the school at the time. Luckily, another girl had also moved from Adelaide and they shared a room. Michelle cried often during the first 6 months, as she missed her family terribly and her brother was only 2 years old at that time. She remembers being quite exhausted adjusting to her new routine of half a day of dance and then half a day of academic learning, due to the physical demands, but also to not having any knowledge of how best to fuel her body to perform. She would go on to complete her high school at the VCA and then progress to the tertiary course, where she also studied drama.

After completing her studies, she secured a job with a Canberra-based dance company and enjoyed steady work for 3 years. When the company disbanded, however, she experienced the reality of working life as a dancer: not knowing what is next, never being quite sure and only having work for a couple of months at a time. She got used to this uncertainty and work seemed come up fairly consistently prior to the birth of her first child.

Michelle has worked nationally and internationally, including in Japan, the United States, Russia, Mongolia, China, Finland, Brussels, Germany, Singapore, Hong Kong and France. She is a recipient of the Australian Postgraduate Award (Industry) Scholarship and several Victorian Green Room Awards; she has also been nominated for the Helpmann and Australian Dance Awards.

Michelle is particularly proud of her own production, *In Plan*, which premiered at the Castlemaine Festival in 2015 and for which she was runner up in the Australian Dance Awards. *In Plan* told the story of two families escaping from East Germany and reoriented the audience's physical experience through a uniquely designed raised platform. Audience members were asked to lie down on their backs to view the dance performance, which was reflected in a mirror above them; the dancers under the platform used a range of illusions and techniques that gave the performance an almost magical feel.

Michelle's husband worked on this production with her. He had studied at the VCA at the same time as Michelle and although they had not met at school, their lives had intersected regularly across the years. When they finally met, it then seemed so obvious. "Having a partner who understood the lifestyle, because he worked in dance companies and the circus, made life a lot easier. Doing the work I loved allowed me to see the world and do amazing things and this can be punishing for the people left behind."

Michelle's experience in the arts in Australia is that it is quite ageist, and gets harder to be funded as you get older. "It is very competitive securing funding and there is not a lot of money to go around." Many organisations are trying to do the right thing and support independent artists. The impacts of COVID-19 have sparked independent artists to come together to collaborate and support each other, to think more critically and long term about how people can sustain a living. Relying on grant applications and the associated limitations just isn't enough. Most people secure other jobs to be able to pursue their art.

Undertaking her master's in dance and moving to regional Victoria, as well as raising two children, all impacted Michelle's work. During this time, she became more recognised as a "maker" rather than a performer and the momentum of work slowed down. She started doing more teaching and working in the disability sector with dance. She always found more meaning in helping people through dance as opposed to purely entertaining.

She has deliberated over many years about the next stage in her career, questioning how long she can sustain a living in dance, especially as she gets older. She has been exploring ways to adapt her skills to a health-care setting. A research project that she undertook with the Royal Children's Hospital, Melbourne, explored using dance to help patients confined to a hospital bed. This provided insight into how she might be able to use what she knows and loves in a new way.

Ready to learn something, undertake a new challenge and for mental stimulation, she has begun a master's in play therapy with Deakin University. The prospect of studying something very new and outside of her current field of expertise was daunting. Her fellow students all have health-sector experience and some medical knowledge, so she felt a little overwhelmed at first. However, her commitment and her willingness to learn have enabled her studies and she is doing quite well so far. She still thoroughly enjoys choreography and performing, and describes a recent rehearsal where she experienced a deep state of flow, improvising for 4 hours continuously, unaware of the time passing. This is an example of how an activity can be so enjoyable that the reward is purely in the act itself. Michelle hopes to find these experiences of flow in her new career, combining her dance experience and newly gained knowledge helping children and teenagers through the therapeutic power of play.

Michelle is, and always will be, a creative and a performer, and her story demonstrates how as life and circumstances change, you can continue to find ways to be satisfied with the work that you do and incorporate opportunities for flow into your everyday work. Her story also shows there's multiple career paths for most people that provide for satisfaction and enjoyment. She's in the process of making a significant change to a very new career, but also finding ways to incorporate all of her strengths and capabilities in a new way. Tackling her second master's was a challenge and, although highly motivated, she has had to work on her confidence to succeed. She has done this through small steps, proving to herself that she is capable. As with any change, she still experiences uncertainty and questioning. Perhaps her experience of living with uncertainty, being a creative in the arts world, means it is something that she is used to and she knows how to persevere and see where it takes her. She also has the support of her partner, who she describes as her soulmate, and his encouragement certainly enables her to continue to make this next exciting change.

26 FRANCES

Frances started her legal career in South Africa in 1987, graduating from the University of Cape Town and joining a law firm straightaway, where she completed 2 years of articles and then stayed for the best part of 15 years.

Appointed as a director relatively early on, her specialty was workplace relations, and she effectively established that department. The practice subsequently merged with a Johannesburg firm and became one of the top commercial law firms in South Africa. "When we decided that we were going to move to Australia, it was a matter of considering the next stage of my legal career. I had to requalify in certain areas and started that study from South Africa through Deakin University."

Moving to Australia in October 2001 with her husband and two young children, they didn't have jobs lined up or know where to live. "I quickly found a job with one of the top-tier Melbourne law firms and stayed for 2 years. The big focus at the time was our children, who were just 2 and 4, and finding suitable childcare. We ended up hiring a nanny who was wonderful, but what I found quite difficult was not having enough contact with them. Much of my salary was ending up with the nanny and I felt I was missing out."

Resigning from her job, she started a master's at the University of Melbourne. She approached various law firms directly, proposing that she could work for them and was surprised that one of them actually said yes, considering she only had 10 hours a week to dedicate to work, as her youngest was still in kindergarten. The partner who hired her agreed to start small and grow from there. She increased her contribution to work in line with school hours and eventually became full-time. "That partner had given me an amazing opportunity to *have a go* and I was very grateful. Unfortunately, he ended up having quite a bad stroke at a very young age and I really missed him at the firm. I stayed on for about another year, and then an opportunity came up to go in-house at General Motors. What excited me about the role was that I had not worked in-house before and I really liked the idea of being at the coalface. I enjoy being closely connected to a client's business and being able to influence strategy and decision-making. I'm passionate about the workplace and manufacturing as well."

An early memory for Frances was going to a potato chip factory and watching the "humble potato transform into a packet of chips like magic. I've always loved cars. I had my own toy cars when I was little and Barbie dolls too, but I certainly had my cars and enjoyed playing car games with some of the local boys. The combination of being able to apply law with my interests and an opportunity to engage in something different all attracted me to join."

Before she accepted the role, she had done her due diligence and understood that it was quite a tenuous situation for automotive manufacturing. "I wasn't looking for a job for life, I was looking for an experience where I could add value and learn. Irrespective of how long it lasted, it was going to be interesting."

One of her many proud achievements was working on the enterprise bargaining variation. "It was a really exciting period of time, an adrenaline-driven 6 weeks under a lot of scrutiny by the media. There were always questions back then about what this meant for the future of Holden and working with a team to get the agreement together, navigating through some of the tricky aspects, and having the agreement voted on and then approved by the Fair Work Commission was a sense of tremendous satisfaction. Also, the last enterprise agreement negotiation occurred in 2014 with separation packages and negotiating a way forward with six unions. Even though it was only one agreement, the complexity made it interesting, it was incredibly long and included a number of legacy items/entitlements that people were very focused on retaining. I would also comment on the cohesive teams, and the sense of family right across Holden. There was certainly a very close connection between everyone driven by the business and the brand and the desire to keep the brand in Australia. That created a sense of family and of unity."

Frances described how the culture within the legal team was also a very united one. As a team, they got on well together, enjoyed each other's company and would do fun activities like learning to cook French cuisine and going on a "Hot Lap" with top supercar driver, Garth Tander. That created a sense of togetherness and fun to balance out the hard work. Many people were "car people," so Frances felt pretty comfortable with all of them, being a car fan herself. "The people were really decent, positive, encouraging and nice to work with, so the culture was an encouraging, positive one."

It was a seismic moment when they announced closure; everyone took a deep breath and thought, "Well, what now?" Others, like Mitsubishi, had reinvented themselves and that was what Holden would need to do. As manufacturing was closing, it was logical that her role would eventually go and she was quite open-eyed about it.

An opportunity arose in her last year at Holden where a speaker at a conference in Sydney was unable to attend and offered the opportunity to her network. Frances immediately volunteered to step in, not really knowing what the speech was about. It ended up being for the International Bar Association (IBA) global conference in Sydney, which led to many more engagements. In fact, she's now a committee member of the IBA's Diversity and Equality Law Committee.

Frances encourages others to look for opportunities to stretch their wings and to take advantage of things. "Even if you're unsure, perhaps look at it as part of acquiring skills." She realised in about May 2017 that her role was going at the end of that year, so she had a fairly decent amount of time to get herself out in the marketplace and see what she could create. Ultimately, she found a role in the public service that she thought would be an interesting challenge and where she could contribute. At the time of publication, Frances holds the position of Assistant Victorian Government Solicitor for Workplace Relations and Occupational Safety.

She freely shares that there are quite a few things in her life that she finds important outside of work. There's an important spiritual dimension to her life that she draws a lot of strength from. There's also her family, close friends and music as a vital part of her existence, providing a lot of enjoyment. One thing that she does admit probably needs to feature more is sleep, because sleep is a strategy for being able to cope with things.

She credits her experience at Holden with helping her to build skills in thinking on her feet, dealing with a quickly changing set of circumstances and having the right mindset to deal with whatever comes her way. She also learnt to be quite resourceful, as the legal team at Holden didn't have massive resources at their disposal, so they had to be fairly inventive and think outside the square. Another key thing she learnt from her own leader, Fiona, was to find ways to say "yes."

From a young age, Frances adopted an openness to continuously learn and to reflect on different kinds of opportunities, as well as to adapt to change. To anyone facing change, she'd say: "It's a great opportunity. Don't see it as a negative. I don't want to sound too trite about it, but change is actually a good thing. Change is an opportunity for improvement or for something new, for growth, or development. You need to know the 'why' behind something before you start embarking on a change so that it will sustain you when it's not going so well or where you hit a few potholes in the road. Our move from South Africa to Australia was not the easiest of things to do with two young kids, but what drove us was, that we were doing it for a good reason. I also think when you're looking at making a change it's best not to over-analyse things. Just understand that there's a good reason to be making the change and get on and do it. If you don't want to make that change, the flip side is to make the best of where you are. You just don't want to be in a state of discontent and inertia. Probably the worst place to be is unhappy and not moving anywhere, because then you're stagnating.

Accept where you are, and make the best of it. I know this sounds easy to do, but it's actually much harder in practice than it sounds. I could be a better student of my own coaching and agonise over decisions less."

"No one's perfect and our imperfections make us who we are, but we can always do better. And we can always try and uncover what matters in life. Sense of purpose is what drives us, so get back to that 'why' question. I've become increasingly conscious of the importance of why you do something and the importance of doing things for others, which I believe is what we're really here for. To influence others in a positive way, in whatever we do. We live lives that are complex and not perfect; however, we can try to see beyond our individual circumstances, that we are here to help others and play a meaningful role. It is a great privilege to do be able to do that. You draw a lot of energy and positivity from it and the more you focus on those things, the more you feel your wheels moving and you're getting somewhere. You don't need to know where the destination is, but you're involved and contributing and that's what's important."

While Frances' career has always been in law, she has had a varied and interesting career. She advocates for movement over stagnation, and for continuing to learn and grow whether you stay in your current job or make a change. Frances provides a great example of being really clear on your priorities in life and what is important to you. For her, it is her family, her spirituality, her passion for music and her career. Meaning and purpose feature prominently for Frances, as well as having a positive impact in all that she does both in her personal and professional life. What you maybe can't hear from her story is her warm nature, generous smile and passion for life in general. I personally have learnt a lot from working with her and from staying connected to her since leaving Holden and I hope you can take inspiration from her wise words.

27 ED

Ed started with Holden in 2007 and when he joined, he was told he was *lucky* to be a permanent employee, as most positions were being offered only on contract. There was a lingering unshakable air of uncertainty with constant change and with General Motors having moved a lot of work back to North America, which impacted projects in Australia.

He remembers the announcement of the closure of manufacturing very well. He was standing at the front of the Atrium (a large, very white, open space in the foyer of the Australian headquarters building in Salmon Street, Port Melbourne). Being an open atrium and surrounded on two sides by corridors on the first and second floors, it was a space where all employee meetings were held and people would fill the ground floor and the corridors above. Few were completely surprised that manufacturing was to close in Australia but some were a bit more optimistic about timing. "It was actually a relief to know what was going to happen. It wasn't happy relief; it was still sad. I really enjoyed my time there, the people I worked with and the different roles I had."

That being said, even though employees were informed that closure was happening, there was still no specific timeline as it would be a rolling closure and impact many functions across the business. It was almost 12 months to the day of the announcement (December 2014) when the first round of reductions took place in Victoria and Ed's job and many others were made redundant.

He described it as disappointing, working for a manufacturing company, where you put your heart and soul into something, and the end result was a national sales company. There had been a constant change in leadership, and with every change, a change in company direction. "So, there was never really stability. After the announcement, a lot of people became disengaged because they were looking for a way out, or they were just unsure of what to do."

Ed reflects that maybe because he was younger at the time, it didn't really faze him. He still went about doing his job as normal. It was only when the transition/people-support programs started being rolled out and voluntary redundancies had progressed to compulsory that he started to think about what he was going to do. He began to feel concerned that he hadn't really used any of his formal qualifications in science and industrial chemistry for over 7 years since joining Holden.

Ed had been applying for jobs in the lead up to his redundancy but didn't find anything. He sat down with his partner. She was heading back to England in February for a friend's wedding, which he'd also been invited to. He made the decision to take January off as a bit of a summer break and go traveling. "I guess I was a bit in denial and postponing thinking about stuff for the first few months. When I got back to Australia, everyone I knew was going off to work, Monday to Friday, and I was sitting there twiddling my thumbs. I didn't realise at the time that I was getting a bit depressed. My partner was really helpful, not just from an emotional standpoint, but in getting me motivated and helping me apply for jobs, which I hadn't had to do for the better part of 10 years. I mean, when I applied for Holden, it was a one-page resumé. Now, you have to write a mini essay on key criteria. It was a real change."

Ed had a number of close friends who knew that things were tough for him and they made time to catch up socially and talk. Not just focus on the fact that he was looking for work, but also on other interests, trying to keep a balance.

Getting a base version of his resumé and being able to adapt it to each application certainly helped. He also built what he describes as database of examples of his experience that he could draw from.

Looking back on this time of change, there is a lot that Ed wishes he'd known back then. Up until his redundancy, he'd succeeded in securing pretty much every job he'd applied for. It took some adjustment to realise that's probably not the norm in this day and age. He originally started out thinking he'd apply for one job, but his partner encouraged him to apply for 5 to 10 jobs and each application could take hours to write. He realised he had to have a bit more mental fortitude in terms of looking for a job, as that in itself was a full-time job.

This job-seeking time affected him physically and mentally. He was quite depressed about the whole situation and was getting a lot of nice "thanks, but no thanks" rejection letters. He had been told by his career coach, friends and family that he had a lot of great skills that were transferable and consequently he was motivated to look for a role outside the automotive industry. But whenever he interacted with a recruiter, their response was "we don't really have anything in automotive."

One of his colleagues had secured a role with Ford and let him know about a contract opportunity. The application process was slow, but he finally got the job. It ended up being a 9-month gap between finishing at Holden and starting his new role at Ford.

This was a difficult time for Ed; his first personal experience of mental ill health and struggling to find a job. "There were some days where you just don't want to go through this again. I'm sick and tired of looking and I'm sick and tired of doing this. And I wasn't doing it every day, I still went out and was social." He especially credits his now wife for getting him through this, as well as his close family and friends.

For anyone facing redundancy, or wanting to make a change, Ed's advice is "not to give up. There were a lot of times when I just felt like throwing in the towel, and maybe I could get a job stacking shelves or something. I think also, don't be afraid to try new things. Yes, I'm still working in automotive, but I ended up getting a role in finance, which is something that I'm not technically qualified in. It's not traditional finance, it's for production and development. So still very much linked with automotive. But everyone I work with has an accounting or business degree. I'm actually just moving out of that role back into an engineering role in the business office dealing with resourcing, so a different change all over again."

Probably one his biggest regrets is being stubborn and prideful. Originally, he dealt with a lot of stuff on his own and with his wife and personal network. "So that's probably one of the stupidest things I've done." He felt he should have been asking for help and willing to seek advice from everyone. "It might not apply directly to you and it might be conflicting advice, but it just helps to build your knowledge base on options of what you could be doing."

Ed's parting words point to the power of networking and expanding your options of what you could be doing. While he has remained in automotive, he has done many and varied jobs and continued to change and move his career forward. No matter how long it takes to land another job after redundancy, it is still a challenging experience that requires grit, support from others and self-care. His close relationships helped him through the low points and sustained and motivated him to keep going. It was a referral through his network that eventuated in his move to Ford. Through two more job changes at Ford, he has proven that he now has the skills to make a change and he continues to learn and develop new skills and knowledge. I was humbled interviewing Ed, hearing his honesty and openness. Hopefully his story normalises the challenges that can occur and the ability to advance through setbacks; that it is a matter of *when*, not *if*, you will land that next opportunity and that you are capable of making a change.

28 AMALIA

The granddaughter of Greek immigrants, I worked in my parents' curtain manufacturing business while I went to university, which later led to a job with a fabric wholesaler in customer support and sales. After a couple of years, I secured an administration role with a large successful recruitment firm and was then promoted to recruitment consultant for a few years. While I enjoyed the work, I did not enjoy the pressure to sell and the priority focus on revenue over value delivered. I moved into an internal recruitment role with PricewaterhouseCoopers Consulting, which was later bought by IBM. I would end up spending almost 10 years there, progressing through a range of human resources and learning leadership roles, often with a strong focus on career and capability development.

In 2008, I was fortunate to become pregnant with my second child. At the time, I was working for one of the best leaders I had ever worked for. At 11 weeks' pregnant, I contracted Guillain-Barré syndrome, a rare condition in which the immune system attacks the nerves, likely caused by an infection. Unable to have the required pain medication, I lived with chronic pain and was bedridden for 6 months. My partner was an amazing support and took leave to care for me and our 2-year-old. Saved financially by IBM employee income protection insurance, physically by modern medicine and emotionally by family support,

I was extremely lucky to make a full recovery and have a healthy baby girl.

This traumatic experience did not have the impact I would have anticipated. I had missed working; and fortunately my partner had thoroughly enjoyed being a stay-at-home Dad. Once I was well enough, and my daughter old enough, I returned to full-time work, keen to progress my career. My partner cut back his hours to part-time.

In 2010, IBM was reducing the number of HR staff in high-cost countries, like Australia. A small number of people needed to be made redundant. I was told by one of the senior leaders that I "was not on the list"; however, she "knew how unhappy I was and that I was ready for a change. If I could see this as an opportunity, then someone else in the team who desperately wanted to stay, could." I asked for 24 hours to think about it, and the next day said "yes." Although it was definitely time to make a change and it was my choice to do so, it was still an emotional experience. It felt like a form of rejection, and a daunting leap into the unknown.

My next role was in government, working for the Victorian Department of Transport. When the State Government Savings Initiative came in, I had to cut almost my entire team and would lose all my budget, and therefore included myself as one of the redundancies. Luckily, I was approached to head up HR for a property developer and real estate firm at the same time as leaving. The people were great, and as HR was new there, they appreciated what I delivered. After a large acquisition of another firm, who already had an HR department, I realised that while I loved the people, the work was not what I wanted to be doing and again was able to present a case that the HR team of the acquisition business was better placed to remain and therefore my role should be made redundant. (Can you see a pattern yet?)

Shortly after, I secured a role with General Motors Holden to support the closure of manufacturing and help the business transform into a national sales company. This is probably the job in my career that I was most drawn to, almost called to do. Holden is such an iconic brand, and I later found out that my grandfather had worked there for a brief time during World War II. I clearly remember thinking that if something crappy is going to happen to a lot of good people, then there needs to be someone who actually cares about people and wants the best outcome for them to lead that program.

I worked closely with my counterpart, Sally, who was based in Adelaide, and Denis, a long-serving business partner who is probably one of the nicest guys I've ever worked with. The three of us were the designers, creators and implementors of the Holden Transition program which supported almost 3000 workers into gainful employ-ment. Naturally, as manufacturing closed, there was less of a need for two people to lead the transition (Sally and myself); therefore my role was made redundant.

I then joined one of Australia's big four banks, in a leadership role in learning. The money was great and flexibility was no issue. At first, things were enjoyable. I had a wonderful team, interesting work and company commitment to the projects in our remit. Unfortunately, not long into the role, it became difficult for me to muster enthusiasm. The Sunday-night dread started earlier on Sunday afternoons, and my ineffective and unhealthy coping strategy of a few wines in the evening moved from two nights a week to four. The problem was that I had come from an organisation with a product I connected to and was proud of, where I had a feeling of satisfaction and achievement that the work I was doing was helping many people. I had moved to an organisation where I struggled to get excited about the product, and I was so far removed from the employees, working in the head office function and acting as a back-office expert. I had no sense of helping people, despite the data confirming that what my team was delivering was helpful and being used.

My partner had suggested that he use his leave and take a year off to support me while I took on the role with the bank. Being part-time in the police force had pretty much put an end to him progressing any further in his career and he was keen to support me. It was during that year that we found a house 50 minutes from Melbourne, in a town in the Macedon Ranges. We fell in love with the house, luckily found a great school for our two girls and negotiated a long settlement, so we could move in time for the girls to start the new school year.

Unfortunately, in the months leading up to our move, I hadn't noticed a lot of little signs that my partner was actually suffering from mental health problems. Not sure how I missed it, but maybe you can relate to that feeling of realising that there were plenty of signs and it all makes sense in retrospect, but you just didn't see it at the time. He was later diagnosed with post-traumatic stress disorder, which was related to his almost 30-year career with the police force.

While the financial responsibility had always been mine in our relationship, and I was the primary breadwinner, this was even more prevalent now. I felt this responsibility and self-imposed pressure even more. When an opportunity came to leave the bank, with a fancy-sounding title and to earn the same income, I jumped at it. Unfortunately, it was to be another lesson that great money and a fancy title doesn't bring satisfaction and meaning.

I was under enormous pressure trying to keep the family functioning, move house and organise everything that goes with that. I eventually told my new boss what I was dealing with. Being over an hour away, working in the city, left me feeling particularly vulnerable and concerned. When I travelled a lot or was under pressure to stay late, it was really tough. I had to check in at home to make sure everyone was ok.

At breaking point, in another job I hated and a challenging home life, I got help from my local GP and a wonderful psychologist. I prioritised my own health and happiness, started Pilates and yoga, lost weight, and managed to negotiate a separation from my employer. Luckily for me, a business transformation had significantly changed my role, entitling me to negotiate a payout to leave.

Towards the end of 2019, I started my own business, with the intention of doing more of the work I love and learning more along the way. The COVID-19 pandemic meant that 2020 was challenging, and while I had a few loyal clients, a lot of work that was committed to vanished overnight. So far, 2021 is looking promising with a few contracts in the pipeline. I'm back to prioritising my health and happiness and fulfilling my purpose of *helping people*, in whatever way I can, including writing this book!

There are a number of ways I can fulfil that purpose and find meaning in the work I do. Hopefully that will continue to be in my own business, but if after a while those circumstances have to change because of my other life priorities, then I can still find a way to use my strengths, capabilities, find meaning, fulfil my purpose, and gain satisfaction and enjoyment from the work I do.

There's also more than one path for *you* to be happier with your career that works in tandem with your other priorities in life. I'm so grateful you've spent some of your precious time reading this book and completing some, if not all, of the activities. I hope that you've been uplifted, inspired and delighted as you make your way towards understanding your options (perhaps there are more than you anticipated!). Be clear on what you need and what you want, and take action to achieve your goals, not only in your work but in the rest of your life, more broadly. Sharing this journey with the right support crew will strengthen those bonds and help you lift even higher. You're hopefully now more confident, not only in your own capabilities, but also in your ability to make a successful change to your career or job. And remember that you can continue to make these kinds of changes again, whenever you want or need to do so.

You now have the tools and strategies to secure more enjoyable and satisfying work and you'll soon be reaping the positive benefits of that in regards to your happiness and wellbeing. I wish you luck on your journey, but you don't need it. Effort combined with these tools and your capabilities. . .

"You know what you know. . . Oh, the places you'll go!"

ACKNOWLEDGEMENTS

There are many people who contributed to the creation of and inspiration for this book.

People humbled me with their generosity with their time, sharing their stories and keen insights that formed the research for this book through the interviews. A special thank you to Phong Nguyen, who was the first interview subject and helped me rally many others to contribute. I would have loved to include more of the stories, perhaps in another format and for another purpose. However, a massive thank you to everyone I interviewed. To Mark, Jo and Jason, some of the key senior leaders at Holden, and to Amanda, Andrew, Joe, David, Louisa, Narelle, Martha, Sally, Toni, Michael and Paul, thank you.

To the people whose stories made it into the final edit for the book, Sandy, Michelle, Jeff, Frances and Ed, thank you for your honesty, bravery and willingness to share.

To my friends who read early versions of the first few chapters: Toni, Anthony and Eleni, to Becky for your publishing advice and to Barb for reading the book cover-to-cover for the final polish. Your insights and suggestions were truly valuable. To my editor, Melanie, who challenged me to change the structure and almost completely re-write this book. Overwhelmed at first, we were united in making this as helpful as possible to many people and with your help I hope we have achieved that. Thank you for your honesty, your passion and ability to understand my intentions that were sometimes not clear through my words.

Lastly and most importantly I want to thank my beautiful daughters Penny and Ellie to whom I am grateful for the love, joy, laughter and sometimes tears they bring to my life. Thank you for being you. To Jonathan for your belief and support and to my parents for raising me to optimistically believe almost anything is possible with effort and hard work.

I am forever grateful and appreciative of all your help.

REFERENCES

Part One: Self and Others

Chapter 1: Are You Ready?

1. Maarten Vansteenkiste, Richard M. Ryan and Bart Soens. 2020. "Basic Psychological Need Theory: Advancements, Critical Themes, and Future Directions." *Motivation and Emotion,* 44(1), 1.
2. Ken Paller and Satoru Suzuki, "Consciousness." In R. Biswas-Diener & E. Diener (Eds.) Noba (2019) textbook series: Psychology. Champaign, IL: DEF publishers. http://noba. to/5ydq3tgk.
3. John Gerzema and Michael D'Antonio. 2017. "The Athena Doctrine: Millenials Seek Feminine Values in Leadership," *Journal of Leadership Studies,* 10(4), 63.

Chapter 2: Pause, Play and Rewind

1. Stuart Brown. 2010. *Play: How it Shapes the Brain, Opens the Imagination and Invigorates the Soul.* Brunswick, VIC, Australia: Scribe Publications.

Chapter 3: The Whole Picture

1. Ed Diener, Robert A. Emmons, Randy J. Larsen and Sharon Griffin. 1985. "The Satisfaction with Life Scale," *Journal of Personality Assessment,* February, 49(1), 71–75.
2. Nansook Park and Martin Seligman, 2013. "Christopher M. Peterson (1950–2012)," *The American Psychologist,* 68(5), 403.
3. The Royal Melbourne Hospital/5 Ways to Wellbeing. n.d. "Connect". https://5waysto wellbeing.org.au/5-ways/connect/.
4. Barbara Fredrickson. 2011. *Positivity, Groundbreaking Research to Release Your Inner Optimist and Thrive.* London, England: Oneworld Publications. 22.

Chapter 4: Driving Decisions

1. Shalom H. Schwartz. 2012. "An Overview of the Schwartz Theory of Basic Values," *Online Readings in Psychology and Culture,* 2(1).
2. Brené Brown. 2018. "Operationalizing Your Organization's Values," September 23. https://daretolead.brenebrown.com/operationalizing-your-orgs-values/.
3. Shalom H. Schwartz. op. cit. 16.

Chapter 5: Flow

1. Mihaly Csikszentmihalyi. 1990. *Flow: The Psychology of Optimal Experience*. New York NY: Harper and Row. 2.
2. ibid.

Chapter 6: Strengths

1. Robert Biswas-Diener, Todd B. Kashdan and Gurpal Minhas. 2011. "A Dynamic Approach to Psychological Strength Development and Intervention," *The Journal of Positive Psychology*, 6(2), 109.
2. Shalom H. Schwartz. op. cit.
3. Christopher Peterson and Martin Seligman. 2004. *Character Strengths and Virtues, A Handbook and Classification*. New York, NY: Oxford University Press.

Chapter 8: Growth

1. Carol S. Dweck. 2006. *Mindset: The New Psychology of Success*. New York, NY: Random House. 6.
2. Mary Forehand. 2005. "Bloom's Taxonomy: Original and Revised" In M. Orey (Ed.) *Emerging perspectives on learning, teaching and technology*. CreateSpace Independent Publishing Platform.

Chapter 9: Meaning and Purpose

1. Amy Wrzeniewski, Clark McAuley, Paul Rozin and Barry Schwartz. 1997. "Jobs, Careers and Callings: People's Relations to their Work." *Journal of Research in Personality*, 31(3), 21–33.
2. Israel Selvanayagam. 2018. "*The Human Quest for Meaning, Theories, Research and Applications,* Edited by Paul T.P. Wong". *Implicit Religion: Journal of the Centre for the Study of Implicit Religion and Contemporary Spirituality,* 20(4), 437–41.
3. ibid.
4. Simon Sinek. 2019. "How Great Leaders Inspire Action." TEDxPuget Sound, Newcastle, WA, video 17:49.
5. Viktor E. Frankl. 1986. *Man's Search for Meaning: An Introduction to Logotherapy.* 3rd ed. New York, NY: Simon & Schuster. 66.

Chapter 10: Identity

1. Darja Kragt and David V. Day. 2015. "Identity and Identification at Work." *Organizational Psychology Review*, 6(3), 216.
2. Jane E. Dutton, Laura Morgan Roberts and Jeffrey Bednar. 2010. "Pathways for Positive Identity Construction at Work: Four Types of Positive Identity and the Building of Social Resources." *Academy of Management Review*, 35(2), 267.
3. Dan P. McAdams. 2020. "Self and Identity". In R. Biswas-Diener & E. Diener (Eds.) Noba textbook series: Psychology. Champaign, IL: DEF publishers. http://noba.to/3gsuardw.

Chapter 11: Relationships for Support

1. Barbara Fredrickson. 2011. *Positivity, Groundbreaking Research to Release Your Inner Optimist and Thrive*. London, England: Oneworld Publications. 191.

2. Shelly Gable, Harry T. Reis, Emily A. Impett and Evan R. Asher. 2004. "What do you do when things go right? The intrapersonal and interpersonal benefits of sharing positive events." *Journal of Personality and Social Psychology*, 87(2), 228–245.
3. Shelly Gable, Gian C. Gonzaga and Ay Strachman. 2006. "Will you be there for me when things go Right? Supportive responses to positive event disclosures." *Journal of Personal and Social Psychology*, 91(5), 905–906.

Chapter 12: Networks

1. Jane Dutton and Emily Heaphy. 2003. "The Power of High-Quality Connections." In K. S. Cameron, J. E. Dutton and R. E. Quinn (Eds.) *Positive Organizational Scholarship: Foundations of a new discipline*. San Francisco, CA: Berrett-Koehler. 263.

Chapter 13: Place

1. Bradley S. Jorgensen and Richard C. Stedman. 2001. "Sense of Place as an Attitude: Lakeshore Owners Attitudes Toward their Properties." *Journal of Environmental Psychology*, 21(3), 233–234.
2. Marino Bonaiuto, Yanhui Mao, Scott Roberts, Anastasia Psalti, Silvia Ariccio, Uberta Ganucci Cancellieri and Mihaly Csikszentmihalyi. 2016. "Optimal Experience and Personal Growth: Flow and the Consolidation of Place Identity." *Frontiers in Psychology*, 7, 1654.
3. Jacqueline C. Vischer PhD and Mariam Wifi. 2015. "The Effect of Workplace Design on Quality of Life at Work." In Ghozlane Fleury- Bahi, Enric Pol and Scar Navrro (Eds.) *Handbook of Environmental Psychology and Quality of Life Research*, London, England: Springer. Chapter 20.

Chapter 14: Movement

1. Kelly McGonigal PhD. 2020. *The Joy of Movement: How Exercise Helps Us Find Happiness, Hope, Connection and Courage*. New York, NY: Avery Publishing Group.

Part Two: The Job Market

Chapter 19: The Interview

1. Daniel Kahneman. 2012. *Thinking, Fast and Slow*. Harlow, England: Penguin Books. 12.

Chapter 22: If at First You Don't Succeed . . .

1. Angela Duckworth. 2020. *GRIT: The Power of Passion and Perseverance*. Simon & Shuster/ Paula Wiseman Books.
2. Richard S. Lazarus. 1999. "Hope: an Emotion and a Vital Coping Resource Against Despair." *Social Research*, 6, 653.

Printed in Australia
AUHW020823070621
346721AU00011B/80

9 781922 553331